Total Customer Experience

Building Business through Customer-Centric Measurement and Analytics

Bob E. Hayes

BUSINESS OVER BROADWAY
TCE: Total Customer Experience – Building Business
through Customer-Centric Measurement and Analytics
Bob E. Hayes, PhD

Copyright © 2013 by Bob E. Hayes
All Rights Reserved

All rights reserved. This book was self-published by Bob E.
Hayes under Business Over Broadway. No part of this book
may be reproduced in any form by any means without the
express permission of the authors. This includes reprints,
excerpts, photocopying, recording or any future means of
reproducing text.

If you would like to do any of the above, please
seek permission first by contacting me at http://
businessoverbroadway.com

Published in the United States by Business Over Broadway

ISBN 978-0-9892804-2-6

Version 1.0

About the Author

"Science is a way of thinking much more than it is a body of knowledge."

Carl Sagan

Bob Hayes is the author of two books, *Measuring Customer Satisfaction and Loyalty* and *Beyond the Ultimate Question*. He is President of Business Over Broadway and Chief Customer Officer of TCE Lab. Hayes holds a BS from University of Washington and an MA and PhD in industrial-organizational psychology from Bowling Green State University.

He conducts research on the measurement of customer satisfaction and loyalty, identifying best practices for business success and writes (books, blogs and articles) regularly on such topics as customer experience management, analytics and Big Data. He works with companies to help them improve their understanding of their customers.

Contents

Preface

I was able to combine two of my interests for this book. The first interest revolves around understanding customers and what makes them loyal. I have been conducting research in the area of customer satisfaction for over two decades and have been helping companies gain insight using customer data for just as long. My first book, *Measuring Customer Satisfaction and Loyalty*, was published in 1992. Since then, I have released the third edition of that book and wrote another one called *Beyond the Ultimate Question* in 2009.

While industry terms used to describe what businesses do to improve customer satisfaction have changed over time, the basic underpinnings (the variables at play) remain the same. Specifically, I once classified my research and work as part of the field of Customer Relationship Management and Customer Loyalty Management. Even though I do the same thing now as before, I classify my work as part of the field of customer experience management (CEM).

My other interest is about the application of analytics to business data. I love data. I love statistics even more. My relationship with statistics started in college when I took an introductory statistics course in the psychology department at University of Washington. I learned the nuts and bolts of statistics and, through brute force, memorized equations for calculating such things as correlation coefficients and mean square within. Up until then, I only knew statistics superficially. My deep appreciation of the beauty of statistics didn't grow until graduate school. After taking the graduate-level series of statistics in graduate school, the professor asked me to be his teaching assistant for those same classes.

As the TA, I sat in on those courses, not necessarily to take notes, but just to listen and make sure I would be aware of the course content for my office hours. The need to clearly articulate statistical knowledge to graduate students helped me understand and appreciate the value of statistics. Additionally, not distracted by note-taking, I was able to see the big picture of statistics and the power of knowing how to look at data when trying to draw conclusions about the world around us. That experience still influences the way I think.

Over the past few years, I have been researching and writing on topics of interest to me: 1) customer experience management and 2) the use and value of data and analytics. My thoughts on these topics appear in my blog posts and presentations. I drew from this content for the current book.

Every field uses terms that are unique to it and the field of customer experience management is no exception. Because the field of CEM deals with customers' perceptions and attitudes, many of the terms we use tend to describe these unobservable entities. Can we really measure something called "employee engagement?" How about "customer loyalty?" A major problem in this field is the lack of clarity when speaking about these unobservable entities. We throw around terms as if everybody understands what we are saying. The term, "customer loyalty," for example, has many different definitions, depending on whom you ask. For some people, it means retention. For others, it means recommendations. Still others think of it as a feeling akin to love or even a process.

Knowing that your metrics tell you something meaningful is necessary to understand how to improve and transform your business. If customer experience management is to advance our understanding of how businesses succeed, we need to be precise with our measures of customer/employee/partner variables as well as our language we use to describe mental processes. Otherwise, I see this field as providing little, real value to businesses; it will be a passing fad.

I decided to take the self-publishing route for this book. For my prior books, I took the traditional publishing route. While my early publishing experiences were great, much of the process was left to the publisher. A lot has changed in the world since then; now, anybody can create a book using self-publishing tools and resources. Using the do-it-yourself method, I was able to curate and edit content that I had created over the prior two years in about three months into a form I thought worthy of a book. I learned about self-publishing in a book by Guy Kawasaki, *APE Author, Publisher, Entrepreneur*. I highly recommend this book.

Businesses have much data at their disposal. Business leaders who think differently about their business data and how to organize and analyze it outperform those who do not. I offer a perspective on how businesses can integrate and analyze different business data to better understand how to keep customers loyalty: coming back, recommending and opening up more of their pocket book. My hope is that this book will help business leaders, researchers and practitioners use the principles of CEM to transform their businesses, advance the scientific study of the customer and facilitate business improvements, respectively.

It's true. When you need help, all you have to do is ask for it. I used a crowd-sourcing method to review and edit an earlier draft of the book. I simply asked my followers (via my blog, twitter and newsletter) for help in return for a softcopy of the book. I would like to take this time to thank these kind people who spent their precious time to help me. They are (in alphabetical order): John Coldwell; Zac de Silva; Dennis Gershowitz; Tracie Hebert; Maz Iqbal; Sumit Jain; Sam Klaidman; Kishore Lakshminarayanan; Polly LeBarron; Barbara J Maroney, MM; Al Nevarez; Nancy Porte; Andy Rogish;

Dr. Ursula Ron; Ronald Segerstrom; Leanne Smith; Mark Stanley; Chi-Pong Wong; Fred Zimny. Thank you all for your feedback. The book is better because of you.

Also, I would like to give a special thanks to Jeremy Whyte for his assistance in pulling together the case study for Oracle!

I would especially like to thank my family and friends. I am lucky to have such wonderful, supportive people in my life. They are: Lamona, Tom, Mom, Foster, Sherrie, Stephen F., Jonathan, Lauren, Christoper, Joshua, Stephen D., Shannon, Sarah, Bryce, Wade, Stephen K. and Vishal. If I missed anybody, I apologize.

Marissa, here is another book dedication for you. Thanks for taking an interest in my professional life by asking me, at least once a year, "Dad, what do you do?" Maybe this book will help answer that question. You have grown into a beautiful, confident woman and I am proud to be your father. I love you.

Theresa, I am so happy that we stumbled onto each other's paths during our random walk through life. I feel fortunate to be a part of your world and I am a better person just for knowing you. You are unmatched in your strength, empathy, humor, intelligence and beauty. You are the air that I breathe, the water that I drink and the star that lights my way. Thank you for sharing your life with me. I will love you always.

Section 1: The 30,000 ft View

"There is only one boss. The customer. And he can fire everybody in the company from the chairman on down, simply by spending his money elsewhere."

Sam Walton

Customer experience management (CEM) is about understanding and managing the customers' interactions with and perceptions about the company or brand. To support this practice, companies develop or improve upon an existing formal CEM program. The benefits of this program are to help them deliver a better customer experience to optimize customer loyalty.

This section of the book explains, at a very high level, the way to conceptualize these CEM activities into a coherent CEM program framework. I will present CEM program practices of loyalty leading companies. I will introduce the concept of Total Customer Experience (TCE) which stresses understanding both the behaviors and attitudes of customers through the proper application of analytics on business data.

Chapter 1: An Overview of CEM, Analytics and TCE

"The price of light is less than the cost of darkness."

Arthur C. Nielsen

Customer Experience Management

While there are existing definitions of customer experience management, they seem to focus solely on the measurement of customers' perceptions and attitudes about their experience. I believe that customer experience management programs, to be effective, need to consider two major types of customer data: 1) customers' interactions with the company and 2) customers' perceptions of their experience. The following definition of customer experience management reflects this idea.

Customer Experience Management (CEM) is the process of understanding and managing customers' interactions with and perceptions about the company/brand.

Customer Loyalty is our Ultimate Criterion

I think that it is safe to state as a matter of fact that customer loyalty is the key to business growth. Businesses that have customers with higher loyalty (e.g., stay longer, recommend, continue buying, increase share-of-wallet, experience more clicks/views) experience faster growth compared to businesses that have customers who engage in fewer loyalty behaviors. The key to growing one's business, then, is to understand how to improve customer loyalty.

Seemingly disparate fields in the CxM space, whether explicitly or implicitly, focus on increasing customer loyalty (isn't optimizing customer loyalty the goal of any business solution?). These disciplines include:

- Customer Loyalty Management (CLM): is the process of maximizing customer loyalty.

- Customer Relationship Management (CRM): is a strategy for managing a company's interactions with customers, clients and sales prospects.

- Customer Lifetime Value (CVM): is the process of managing each customer relationship with the goal of achieving maximum lifetime profit from the entire customer base.

Businesses Use Different Types of Customer Data to Increase Customer Loyalty

Each discipline focuses on using different types of customer data to increase customer loyalty. Businesses tailor ads that resonate with prospects' *personal values* in order to attract types of customers (yes, some people are just more prone to buy, buy, buy; some are more likely to remain loyal). Businesses target marketing/sales campaigns to specific customers based on customers' *purchase/service history.* Businesses measure different types of customer loyalty via *customer feedback tools* to maximize the lifetime value of customers. It is clear that improving customer loyalty is not solely a service problem. Improving customer loyalty can occur throughout each phase of the customer lifecycle (from marketing and sales to service).

Businesses are already realizing the value of integrating different types of customer data to improve customer loyalty. In my research on best practices in CEM programs, I found that the integration of different types of customer data (purchase history, service history, values and satisfaction) are necessary for an effective CEM program. Specifically, I found that loyalty leading companies, compared to their loyalty lagging counterparts, link customer feedback metrics to a variety of business metrics (operational, financial, constituency) to uncover deeper customer insights. Additionally, to facilitate this integration between attitudinal data and objective business data, loyalty leaders also integrate customer feedback into their daily business processes and customer relationship management system.

Different Types of Customer Data

An effective CEM program provides a comprehensive picture of the customers' **interactions** with the company as well as their **attitudes** about the company (See Figure 1.1). As such, the integration of CRM vendors and Enterprise Feedback Management (EFM) vendors (or, at least, the underlying business processes that support both) makes sense for any CEM initiative. For example, prior research at Siebel Systems found that Siebel customers who had **customer satisfaction measurement associated with their Siebel applications** reported greater gains in **revenue** and **user productivity** compared to Siebel customers with standalone Siebel implementations.

CUSTOMER EXPERIENCE MANAGEMENT

Figure 1.1. CEM is the process of understanding and managing customers' interactions with and perceptions about the company/brand.

The integration of different types of customer data provides a comprehensive picture of the customer, individually and as a group. Integration of customer data allows front-line employees to have immediate access to customer information necessary to resolve specific customer problems. Additionally, senior management can apply analytic techniques to this richer customer data to help understand the causes (operational, constituency) and consequences (financial) of customer satisfaction/loyalty, driving systemic changes that affect large customer segments.

A successful CEM program will help deliver a better customer experience. This goal is accomplished by the proper management of customers' interactions with and attitudes about your product/brand. The combined data set that includes both behavioral and attitudinal metrics is more valuable than the sum of its parts.

The Practice of Customer Experience Management

Customer Experience Management (CEM) is the process of understanding and managing your customers' interactions with and perceptions of your company or brand. The ultimate goal of CEM is to build valuable relationships with customers so they stay with you longer, advocate on your behalf and expand their relationship with you over time.

Customer experience management (CEM) programs (sometimes referred to as Customer Feedback Programs, Voice of the Customer Programs, Customer Loyalty Programs) are used in many of today's businesses. These CEM programs are designed to help them understand the causes and outcomes of customers' attitudes and experiences which, in turn, help them to deliver a great customer experience. The ultimate goal of a CEM program is to optimize customer loyalty, consequently improving business performance (Hayes, 2010).

ChiefCustomerOfficerslooktoindustryprofessionals for help and guidance to implement or improve their CEM programs. These industry professionals, in turn, offer a list of best practices for implementing/running these programs (I'm guessing there are as many of these best practice lists as there are industry professionals). I wanted to create a list of best practices that was driven by empirical evidence. Does adoption of best practices actually lead to more effective programs? How do we define "effective"? Are some best practices more critical than others?

I addressed these questions through a systematic study of CEM programs and what makes them work. I surveyed CEM professionals across a wide range of companies (including Microsoft, Oracle, Akamai) about their CEM program. Participants were asked to indicate if their company's program adopted 28 business practices (e.g., senior executive is champion of CEM program; Web-based surveys are used to collect customer feedback). Additionally, respondents were asked to provide an estimate of their company's customer loyalty ranking within their industry; this question was used to segment customers into loyalty leaders (companies with a loyalty ranking of 70% or higher) and loyalty laggards (companies with a loyalty ranking below 70%). The full study can be found in my book, Beyond the Ultimate Question.

A total of 277 of professionals completed the survey. Results showed why some programs are good (company reports high customer loyalty) and others are not (company reports low customer loyalty). Let us take a look at how loyalty leading companies structure their CEM program (see Figure 1.2.).

Figure 1.2. Components of a Customer Experience Management Program

A CEM program has six major components:

- **Strategy** addresses how companies incorporate CEM into their long-term plans to help achieve its objectives and goals

- **Governance** describes the formal policy around the CEM program: Rules, Roles, Request

- **Business Integration** involves embedding CEM processes/data into other business operations and systems

- **Method** addresses the means by which customer feedback is collected

- **Reporting** addresses analysis, synthesis and dissemination of customer feedback

- **Research** is concerned with how companies provide additional customer insight by conducting deep dive research using different types of customer data

Best Practices in Customer Experience Management

The success of your CEM program depends on how you structure it. In a study examining the differences between loyalty leading companies and loyalty lagging companies, I found that loyalty leaders adopted specific business practices in how they approach CEM (See Figure 1.3). Generally speaking, loyalty leading companies have top executive support of the CEM program, communicate all aspects of the program companywide, and integrate customer feedback to other business data (operational, financial, constituency) to gain deeper customer insights. I will cover these areas in more detail later.

Customer Feedback Program Component	Adoption Rate		
	Loyalty Leaders[1]	Loyalty Laggards	Δ in Adoption Rate
Strategy/Governance	89%	71%	**18%**
Business Integration	86%	59%	**27%**
Method	72%	60%	12%
Reporting	70%	60%	10%
Applied Research	80%	51%	**29%**

Figure 1.3. Loyalty Leaders structure their CEM programs differently than Loyalty Laggards.

Strategy and Governance

Strategy addresses the overarching guidelines around the company's mission and vision regarding the company objectives/goals. Governance addresses the guidelines and rules (how the program is directed); roles and responsibilities (how data are used and by whom); and change requests (how changes to the program are made).

Consider using CEM information to set company strategy and formalize the CEM program so everybody knows the rules of the program and their responsibilities. A customer culture is created by effective *and* consistent communications about the customers and their needs. Use actual voice of the customer to drive interest in your CEM program. Loyalty leaders include customer metrics in their executive dashboards and incorporate these same metrics into incentive compensation programs.

Business Integration

Business Integration addresses how the company incorporates CEM processes and data into business operations. Loyalty leaders incorporate CEM metrics into executive dashboards and use them for compensation decisions. You might consider consolidating all sources of customer feedback using an Enterprise Feedback Management (EFM) vendor. I do not see a lot of differences across different EFM vendors as they each offer pretty much the same set of solutions. The key is to find an EFM vendor who knows that CEM is more than just an adoption of their technology. It is about people and processes (and other technology), too, and how their technology addresses your unique needs.

The next step would be to combine the attitudinal data (EFM data) with Customer Relationship Management (CRM) data to get a complete picture of the customer.

Combining these two types of customer data increase the value of the customer data by allowing you to see a more comprehensive picture of your customers. This holistic understanding of what you do to the customer and what she thinks/feels about your company will help you find deeper customer insights you could not find in any single data source. Finally, be sure to communicate all aspects of your CEM program to the entire company and deliver content that matches the needs of the recipient. The content for these types of communications would include program goals, policy changes, governance rules and feedback results, to name a few.

Method and Reporting

CEM programs require a solid understanding of customers' perceptions about your company. The Method of the CEM program addresses how customer feedback is collected and what gets measured. CEM leaders acquire feedback through many different channels, including social media, structured surveys and brand communities. Additionally, companies collect different customer metrics, including satisfaction with different touch points, including product quality, service quality and others, customer loyalty, and customer sentiment. Not surprisingly, loyalty leaders employ the power of the Web to collect customer feedback. As more and more consumers access the Web, loyalty leading companies follow suit and utilize the power of the Web as the vehicle ng with their customers.

leals with how customer feedback data
ynthesized and disseminated throughout
the company. When reporting customer feedback, focus
on both the individual-level reporting and segment-level
reporting. This dual micro/macro approach ensures
you are able to quickly address a specific problem for a
particular customer (e.g., micro approach) and deal with
common problems for large customer segments (e.g.,
macro approach). In the latter approach, be sure to use
appropriate statistical analysis to uncover the reasons
why customers are loyal or disloyal.

Applied Research

Research addresses how the company gains additional
customer insight through deep dive analyses of customer
data. Loyalty leaders combine metrics across different
data sources (e.g., customer feedback, operational,
financial) to get a better understanding of the causes and
consequences of customer satisfaction and loyalty.

Loyalty leaders link CEM metrics to three data
sources. Financial data are linked to CEM metrics
to determine the value of the CEM program. Loyalty
leaders also link operational metrics to CEM metrics to
understand how, for example, call center metrics impact
the customer experience. Finally, loyalty leaders link
constituency metrics (e.g., employee, partner) and CEM

metrics to understand the entire company ecosystem and how different constituencies (e.g., employee and partner) influence the quality of the customer experience.

The Value of Analytics

Businesses are taking advantage of the power of analytics. In 2010, researchers from MIT Sloan Management Review and IBM found that organizations that used business information and analytics outperformed organizations that did not. Top-performing businesses were twice as likely to use analytics to guide future strategies and guide day-to-day operations compared to their low-performing counterparts (see Figure 1.4).

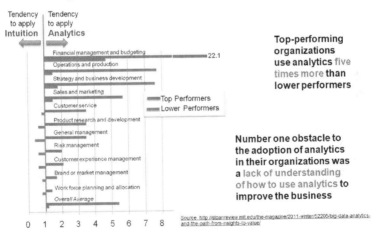

Figure 1.4. Businesses get value from their data using analytics. The graph was recreated. The original image can be found here.

The MIT/IBM researchers, however, also found

that the **number one obstacle to the adoption of analytics in their organizations was a lack of understanding of how to use analytics to improve the business**.

The MIT/IBM researchers also found that six out of 10 respondents cited *innovating to achieve competitive differentiation* as a top business challenge. Additionally, the same percentage of respondents also agreed that their *organization has more data than it can use effectively*. Clearly, companies want to differentiate themselves from the competition yet are unable to effectively use their data to make that happen.

The use of analytics in business is growing and sees much support by business leaders. In a 2012 survey of 600 executives from the US and UK, Accenture found that use of predictive analytics is up threefold (33% in 2012) since 2009. They also found that 68% of the executives rated their senior management team to be highly or totally committed to analytics and fact-based decision making. Additionally, within the last 18 months, two out of three companies have appointed a senior figure (e.g., "chief data officer") to lead data management and analytics.

IBM CEO Virginia Rometty said, when addressing the Council on Foreign Relations 2013 Corporate Conference, **"Data will be the basis of competitive advantage for any organization."** She likened data as "the next natural resource." But while everyone will have access to this natural resource, Rometty continues, "What you do with it will make the difference." She predicts that, for business, "**decisions will be based on predictive analytics and not gut extinct or experience**."

Analytics and Customer Experience Management

According to Accenture, businesses are applying analytics in a variety of different areas that cut across different functional areas like Finance (59%), Customer Service (55%) and Production/Operations (54%) but many with a customer focus. For example, a majority of companies said they are using analytics to improve the customer experience (60%), improve customer retention and acquisition (69%) and monitor competitor performance/activity (65%). To support these different use cases, analytics will necessarily be applied to different kinds of customer data including attitudinal data (e.g., customer satisfaction) and behavioral data (e.g., renews, purchases, clicks).

Improving the ROI for Customer Experience Analytics

Even though businesses are utilizing the power of analytics, they still find it difficult to maximize the return on investment of analytics. In the Accenture study, only 20% of respondents were very satisfied with the business outcomes of their existing analytics programs. The lack of value that executives are experiencing with their analytics may be occurring for a couple of reasons. First, **executives lack clarity regarding the meaning of their analytics**; over half (58%) of executives said they were unclear of business outcomes from the data. Additionally, only thirty-nine percent of the executives said that the data they generate is "relevant to the business strategy".

Second, **the problem of data integration appears to be minimizing the value of analytics.** Half of the executives indicated that data integration remains a key challenge to them. Data are coming from different sources in a variety of forms and companies need analytics to make sense of it all.

Accordingly, to optimize the ROI of customer experience analytics, companies need to focus on three areas:

- **Measure the right customer metrics:** Companies are measuring the wrong things or have gaps in the way they are measuring important variables. Businesses need customer metrics that provide reliable, valid and useful information about the customer relationship (e.g., satisfaction with customer experience, customer loyalty). Applying analytics to reliable, valid and useful customer metrics only serves to improve decision making. Customer metrics that are meaningful (linked to?) to business growth helps executives see the value of the outcome of analytics as they apply to their business.

- **Focus on strategic issues:** Businesses need to use analytics to enhance strategic decision making rather than focusing on tactical issues. This is best accomplished by applying analytics on customer metrics that impact company value (however you define it). By applying analytics on the right customer metrics, businesses will be able to solve strategic business problems (e.g., product development, resource allocation) that really address ROI at an enterprise level (e.g., improve revenue growth, profitability, return on capital, customer loyalty, customer value).

- **Integrate business metrics:** Executives need the correct insights to help in decision making. The right analytics need to help executives gain a cross-functional view of their business data. This cross-functional view is possible only when businesses tie different business data sources together. Integrating metrics from disparate sources is no simple task as different metrics are needed to address different kinds of business questions. For example, addressing questions about how employee metrics impact customer loyalty is a different data integration problem than when addressing questions about how call center metrics impact customer satisfaction.

Total Customer Experience

I use the phrase "Total Customer Experience" and accompanying acronym (TCE) to summarize the marriage of customer experience management (CEM) with different business data (along with appropriate analytics). This holistic view of the customers' attitudes (CEM) about and interactions (other business data) with your company provide a complete picture of your customer. With good measurements and the appropriate application of statistical analyses on these measures, businesses can gain insight into the causes and consequences of customer satisfaction and loyalty and gain a competitive advantage. In the following chapters, I will illustrate how the proper use of measurement and analytics can improve the practice of customer experience management.

Section 2: Strategy and Governance

"Always focus on the front windshield and not the rearview mirror."

Colin Powell

One of the most important characteristics of a successful CEM program is reflected in the executive-level support of the program. Senior executives set company direction, establish organizational rules and implement business processes. Without proper support from the top leadership of the company, any companywide program, including a CEM program, is doomed to failure.

The proper use of business data by senior leadership can help secure the success of the CEM program. Executives use these data to guide the company strategy, allocate resources in areas that matter to the customer and help create a culture in which the customers and their needs come first.

In this section of the book, I will highlight best practices in strategy/governance. I will also present some ideas on how executives can support a customer-centric culture and why senior leaders need to use data rather than opinion when making decisions.

Chapter 2: Best Practices in Strategy and Governance

"Good business leaders create a vision, articulate the vision, passionately own the vision, and relentlessly drive it to completion."

W. Edwards Deming

Strategy and Governance

Strategy reflects the overarching, long-term plan of a company that is designed to help the company attain a specific goal. For customer-centric companies, a major component of their strategy is directed at improving the customer experience.

Because loyalty leaders understand that the formal company strategy and accompanying mission statement set the general culture of the company, they embed the importance of the customer into their mission statements. These customer-centric mission statements instill a set of company values and implicit performance standards about addressing customers' needs. The customer-centric standards shared among the employees act as guidelines with respect to the behaviors that are expected of the employees.

While strategy is necessary to build a customer-centric culture, companies need to create formal policy around the CEM program that supports the strategy. The governance surrounding the CEM program helps foster and maintain a customer-centric culture by operationalizing the strategy (See Figure 2.1).

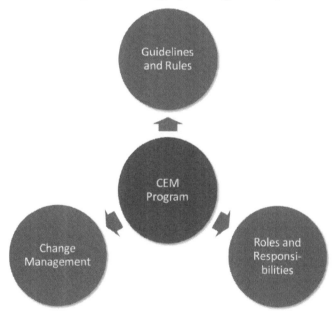

Figure 2. 1. Governance model of a Customer Experience Management Program

Three important areas of governance are:

- *Guidelines and Rules.* These guidelines and rules reflect the set of processes, customs and policies affecting the way the program is directed, administered or controlled. These policies formalize processes around the CEM program and need to be directed at all company's constituents, including board members, senior executives, middle managers, and front-line employees. In a customer-centric company, the work-related behaviors of each of the constituencies are aimed at satisfying customers' needs. As such, customer-centric metrics are used to set and monitor company goals, manage employee behavior and incentivize employees.

- *Roles and Responsibilities.* Need to define and clearly communicate roles/responsibilities across diverse constituency (e.g., board, executives, managers, individual contributor). The definition of the roles and responsibilities need to include how data are used and by whom. Specifically, program guidelines include the way the feedback data from the program are used in different business decision-making processes (resource allocation, employee incentive compensations, account management), each requiring specific employee groups to have access to different types of analytic reports of the customer feedback data.

- *Change Management.* Need to define how changes to the CEM program will occur.

The quality of the policies around the use of the customer feedback data will have an impact on the success of the program. Be clear and precise with how the program will be run. Vague policies regarding how the CEM program is executed, including analytical methods and goals, dissemination of results, and data usage of the customer feedback data, will ultimately lead to suboptimal effectiveness of the program, with limited impact on improving customer loyalty.

Corporate strategy and governance of the CEM program are exhibited in a variety ways by loyalty leaders, from resource allocation in supporting customer initiatives to the using public forums to communicate the company's vision and mission to its constituents. Executive support and use of customer feedback data as well as company-wide communication of the CEM program goals and results helps embed the customer-centric culture into the company milieu. Loyalty leading companies' use of customer feedback in setting strategic goals helps keep the company customer-focused from the top. Additionally, their use of customer feedback in executive dashboards and for executive compensation

ensures the executive team's decisions
by customer-centric issues. A list of
Strategy and Governance is located in

Best Practices	The specifics...
1. Incorporate a customer-focus in the vision/mission statement	Support the company mission by presenting customer-related information (e.g., customer satisfaction/loyalty goals) in the employee handbook. Use customer feedback metrics to set and monitor company goals.
2. Identify an executive as the champion of the customer feedback program	A senior level executive "owns" the customer feedback program and reports customer feedback results at executive meetings. Senior executives evangelize the customer feedback program in their communication with employees and customers. Senior executives receive training on the customer feedback program.
3. Incorporate customer feedback as part of the decision-making process	Include customer metrics in company's balanced scorecard along with other, traditional scorecard metrics. This practice will ensure executives and employees understand the importance of these metrics and are aware of current levels of customer satisfaction/loyalty. Present customer feedback results in company meetings and official documents.
4. Use customer feedback metrics in incentive compensation for executives and front-line employees	Use key performance indicators and customer loyalty metrics to measure progress and set performance goals. Ensure these measures can be impacted by employee behavior. Where possible, use objective business metrics that are linked to customer satisfaction as key performance indicators on which to build employee incentive programs (see Applied Research).
5. Build accountability for customer satisfaction/loyalty goals into the company	Incorporate customer feedback metrics into key performance measures for all employees. Include customer-centric goals in the company's performance management system/processes. Employees set customer satisfaction goals as part of their performance objectives.

Table 2.1. Best Practices in Strategy/Governance

Chapter 3: Creating your Culture

"The single biggest problem in communication is the illusion that it has taken place."

George Bernard Shaw

Customer Experience Management (CEM) programs impact many different constituencies. For example, customers provide feedback in hopes of obtaining better service. Front line employees use customer feedback to help tailor their service calls to improve the customer experience. Still, senior executives rely on customer feedback to effectively allocate resources to improve the customer experience.

To be successful, you need to effectively communicate information about that program to important stakeholders, including employees, partners, and customers. We know that loyalty leading companies communicate customer initiatives throughout the company, from top executives to front-line employees. I found that loyalty leading companies communicate a lot about their CEM program, including its goals, processes and results.

Information Needs

Tailor the communications about the CEM program based on the specific audience's needs. Communication of CEM elements to different stakeholders (employees, partners and customers) serves different purposes. Communications for customers is about optimizing customer loyalty. Communications for other constituencies is about building companywide support for all things customer. You need to communicate two things: 1) you know what's important to customers and 2) you have used customer feedback to make measureable improvements.

What Matters to the Customers

Each employee needs to know which customer touch points are important. Knowing what's important to customers, employees are better equipped to understand what they need to do meet those needs. Senior executives, for example, receive the results that help them make strategic decisions. They require a more holistic look at the data. Front-line employees, on the other hand receive results that help them make immediate decisions. They need information about a specific customer. This micro and macro level of reporting ensures employees understand specific customer concerns as well as customer concerns on a wider scale.

What you are Doing to Improve the Customer Experience

Companies collect customer feedback to make customer experience improvements in areas that matter to the customers. Oftentimes, these improvements come in the form of process and operational changes that impact a large group of customers. Keep track of these operational changes and share them with different constituencies. For each change, keep track of the reasons behind the change (driven by the company or driven by customer feedback) to optimize their use as examples in marketing collateral or customer communications.

The list of changes reflects specific systemic changes designed to improve the customer experience. When creating this list, be specific in your description. Don't just say, "Improved marketing process." Instead, a more precise approach includes the specific problem being addressed, the expected/actual change (if you have data) and the specific customer lifecycle phase that was impacted ("Improved email communications process to ensure customers are not receiving unwanted communications."). To generate this list of changes, you can solicit customer experience improvement examples from your employees or established improvement teams. Keep a list of these accomplishments/changes in a central location to facilitate dissemination of them throughout the company.

Benefits of Sharing

You will receive many diverse benefits from sharing elements of the customer experience management program. Here are four benefits:

- **Improve survey response rates.** Is there anything more frustrating to a customer than not being listened to? Given that customers use their valuable time to provide you feedback to improve your processes, the least you can do is let them know you are listening to them. In your next feedback invitation letter, include the list of specific things your company is doing differently as a result of the customer feedback. Include about 3-5 of these accomplishments in the survey invitation. Sharing information with the customers about how their feedback is impacting how you run your business shows your customers that providing feedback is not a waste of their time; their words result in real and meaningful operational changes.

- **Improve marketing and sales approach.** The list of accomplishments as well as the word clouds, when shared with and digested by the marketing and sales teams, can improve the marketing and sales communications/collateral (especially if responses, in general, reflect high praise).

- **Brand your CEM program.** Customer-centric changes as well as word clouds could be used for branding your CEM program internally and can be included in annual reports when discussing your overall CEM program with employees and company shareholders.

- **Build customer-centric culture**. Sharing customer feedback results across all levels of the company helps keep the customers and their needs in the minds of employees. Listing the ways your company has changed as a direct result of customer feedback helps employees know that senior management is serious about using customer feedback in process improvement efforts. Including these success stories on the company intranet site (e.g., employee portal) can provide the impetus for other employees to think of ways of improving the customer experience.

Summary

Loyalty leading companies share all aspects of their CEM

program to different constituencies. To have a successful CEM program, communicate different aspects of your CEM program to different stakeholders. Two important elements to communicate are: 1) knowledge of customers' needs and 2) the changes you are making to improve the customer experience. The value of these two types of information is seen in improvements in marketing, sales and support, as well as the CEM program itself through increased customer feedback.

Employees need to know the importance of the customer and their needs. Don't do a data dump on the consumers of your CEM data. Share important customer themes across all levels of the company to help employees use the information to make decisions that suit their role.

Chapter 4: It's about People and Processes

"The people make the place."

Benjamin Schneider

Enterprise companies often rely on the use of vendors who help the company collect, analyze and disseminate different sources of feedback (e.g., customers, employees, partners). This process is referred to as Enterprise Feedback Management (EFM). The value that EFM vendors have is their ability to help organizations implement a solution for collecting, analyzing and acting on customer insights.

The use of EFM vendors does not guarantee improvements in the customer experience and customer loyalty. As part of my study on best practices, I found that companies who used third-party survey vendors did not have more loyal customers (Mean = 68th percentile in industry on customer loyalty) than companies who did not use third-party survey vendors (Mean = 65th percentile). Furthermore, of those companies who used third-party vendors, only 60% of the companies were satisfied (20% very satisfied) with them.

CEM Programs are about People, Processes

A CEM program involves more than technology that helps companies capture, analyze and manage feedback. A CEM program contains many components, each impacting the program's effectiveness. To improve customer loyalty, senior executives need to understand that people and processes play a much larger role in the success of a CEM program than the technology used to manage the data.

While each of the six CEM components has best practice standards, the major success drivers are about people and processes and less about technology. Specifically, I found that the top drivers of a company's were the following best practices:

- Customer feedback included in the company's strategic vision, mission and goals.

- Customer feedback results used in executives' objectives and incentive compensation.

- Customer feedback results included in the company/executive dashboards.

- CEM program integrated into business processes and technology (e.g., CRM system).

- All areas of the CEM program (e.g., process and

goals) communicated regularly to the entire company.

- Customer feedback results shared throughout the company.

- Statistical relationships established between customer feedback data and operational metrics (e.g., turnaround time, hold time).

- Applied research using customer feedback data regularly conducted.

- Statistical relationships established between customer feedback data and other constituency metrics (e.g., employee satisfaction or partner satisfaction metrics).

While technology will continue to play a role in improving CEM programs by capturing, aggregating and disseminating customer feedback, it appears that the success of a CEM program is more about people and processes and less about technology. Senior leaders, to have a successful, effective CEM program, need to be cognizant of the importance of each component of their program. Consider how the technology can facilitate people and processes of your program. If you use an EFM vendor for your company, be sure the vendor you choose is more than simply a technology solution, but rather incorporates best practices in people and processes in addition to their technology. Consider using EFM vendors who have professional services or preferred partners who can clearly articulate how the CEM program' data and processes will impact work processes for each company stakeholder, from senior executives to frontline heroes, and how they will address each group's needs.

Chapter 5: Data, Decisions and Biases

"All business proceeds on beliefs, or judgments of probabilities, and not on certainties."

Charles W. Eliot

Senior executives make business decisions based on different types of information. They can use their gut feelings to guide their decisions, they can use data to inform their decisions or they can use both. Executives' decisions can be guided by their prior experiences or an examination of a whole host of business data to help form their decisions.

Opinion v. Data and the US Presidential Election

Let us examine the 2012 US presidential election race and the political pundits who put the race as a tossup. Anybody could win, their narrative went; each candidate had a 50% chance of winning, the probability of a win for either was roughly the same as that of flipping a coin. Nate Silver, a statistician, however, thought that the outcome of the election was far from a 50/50 split. On his site, fivethirtyeight.com, Silver combines the results from many different polls with historical information about prior elections' poll results to reach his forecasts/ predictions about who will win the upcoming election.

Using these data, his statistical model said that Obama had an **85% chance of winning the election** (as of 11/4/2012), far from a tossup. For example, out of 22 **swing-state polls** published on Friday, 19 2012 had Obama in the lead, 1 had Romney in the lead and 2 result in a tie, a very unlikely outcome if the candidates were tied. Of these polls, Obama led in 86% of them.

Pundits even stated negative opinions about Silver's predictions. Joe Scarborough, a pundit on MSNBC.com called Silver a "joke.":

> "Nate Silver says this is a 73.6 (at that time) percent chance that the president is going to win? Nobody in that campaign thinks they have a 73 percent chance — they think they have a 50.1 percent chance of winning. And you talk to the Romney people, it's the same thing. Both sides understand that it is close, and it could go either way. And anybody that thinks that this race is anything but a tossup right now is such an ideologue, they should be kept away from typewriters,

computers, laptops and microphones for the next 10 days, because they're jokes."

Summarizing his response to these attacks, Nate Silver responded:

> "Nevertheless, these arguments are potentially more intellectually coherent than the ones that propose that the leader in the race is 'too close to call.' It isn't. If the state polls are right, then Mr. Obama will win the Electoral College. If you can't acknowledge that after a day when Mr. Obama leads 19 out of 20 swing-state polls, then you should abandon the pretense that your goal is to inform rather than entertain the public."

Using Customer Feedback Data

No matter your political ideology, the polling data were useful in providing insight about the actual election results, a future event. While Silver's exact formula for making predictions remains unknown, what he is essentially doing is averaging many different polling results to make his predictions. His prediction does not say that Obama is certain to win. What it is saying is that **if a candidate has a margin of victory as big as**

Obama has in the polls right now, he wins 85% of the time. It is not a guarantee that Obama will win. But the odds are in his favor. That is all.

Based on what I have seen in this political prognostication battle of opinion versus data, here are some practices that will improve the value of customer feedback data to your organization:

- **Use data to draw your conclusions, especially if there is a preponderance of the evidence about what will happen.** Sure, judgment is important in making important decisions/conclusions, especially in times of uncertainty, but when the data overwhelmingly tell you what is happening, those data trump judgment in their importance to helping you make important decisions about your company.

- **Use hypothesis testing to make business decisions**. Partisan pundits, by definition, will tend to support their side of the argument no matter what the data say. In companies, executives will hold different beliefs about what needs to be done to move the business forward (e.g., where to invest in the company, product development strategies). These beliefs can be tested/supported/disputed using customer feedback data. This process is one of hypothesis testing, using data to rule out alternative explanations for what is occurring in your customer base while supporting other explanations for what is occurring.

- **Use different sources of data to draw your conclusions.** You can be more confident in the result of many studies than any single study alone. Any single poll has a margin of error (sampling error), reflecting the fact that the results are based on a sample of the entire population; that is, the poll might not reflect what is happening in the population. For the presidential election, states, however, have many different polls that study the same outcome. By taking the average of the different polls, you increase your confidence of the prediction/outcome. In the scientific literature, this process is referred to as a meta-analysis (aggregating many different studies of the same topic). A meta-analysis is essentially a study of studies. While there is never 100% certainty about polling data, you can still draw probabilistic conclusions about who will win the electoral vote based on the results of many different samples of likely voters. In business, there are many different sources to tell you the health of the customer relationship, from relationship surveys and transaction-based surveys to social media sites to branded community sites. Looking at different sources of customer feedback will paint a more comprehensive picture of the real health of the customer relationship.

- **Segment your customers.** While the national polling results show a close race, the winner of the popular (national) vote does not determine the winner. The winner of the election is based on the number of Electoral College votes, which are determined state by state. Examining the differences across different customer segments helps you tailor your marketing, sales and service approaches to target specific customer groups' needs. This practice **managing customer segments differently** maximizes the return on investment of your business' resources which helps the **overall performance of the company**.

In the Absence of Data, Everyone is Right

Comparing the pundits with Nate Silver with respect to their respective predictions of the 2012 Presidential

Election outcome, Mr. Silver was clearly the winner, predicting the winner of the presidential election for each state perfectly (yes, 50 out of 50 states) and the winner of the popular vote.

Let's compare how each party made their predictions. While both used publicly available polling data (see Figure 5.2), political pundits appeared to make their predictions based on the results from specific polls. Nate Silver, on the other hand, applied his algorithm to many publicly available polling data at the state level. Because of sampling error, poll results varied across the different polls. So, even though the aggregated results of all polls painted a highly probable Obama win, the pundits could still find particular poll results to support their beliefs.

Monday's Battleground Polls

	Pollster	Monday Poll	Change from Prior Poll
CO	Public Policy Polling	Obama +6.0	Obama +2.0
CO	Lake Research Partners	Obama +1.0	
CO	Ipsos / Reuters (online)	Obama +1.0	Obama +1.0
CO	Keating Research	Obama +4.0	Obama +1.0
FL	Gravis Marketing	tie	Obama +3.0
FL	Ipsos / Reuters (online)	Romney +1.0	Romney +1.0
FL	Angus Reid	tie	Obama +5.0
IA	American Research Group	Romney +1.0	Romney +1.0
MI	Angus Reid	Obama +5.0	Romney +4.0
MI	Mitchell Research	Obama +5.0	Obama +5.0
NH	American Research Group	tie	Obama +2.0
NH	New England College	Obama +4.0	Romney +1.1
NH	Rasmussen Reports	Obama +2.0	Obama +4.0
NV	Public Policy Polling*	Obama +4.0	Obama +1.0
OH	Rasmussen Reports	tie	unchanged
OH	U. of Cincinnati	Obama +1.5	Romney +0.5
OH	Angus Reid	Obama +3.0	Obama +3.0
OH	SurveyUSA	Obama +5.0	Obama +2.0
OH	Ipsos / Reuters (online)	Obama +4.0	unchanged
OH	Gravis Marketing	Obama +1.0	unchanged
PA	Angus Reid	Obama +4.0	Romney +5.0
PA	Gravis Marketing	Obama +3.0	unchanged
VA	Rasmussen Reports	Romney +2.0	Romney +3.0
VA	Mellman	Obama +3.0	Obama +2.0
VA	Ipsos / Reuters (online)	Obama +2.0	Obama +1.0
WI	Angus Reid	Obama +7.0	Obama +2.0
	Average	Obama +2.4	Obama +0.7

* Average of poll with and without third-party candidates.

Figure 5.2. Summary of polling results from fivethirtyeight.com published on 11/6/2012, one day before the 2012 presidential election. Click image to read entire post.

Next, I want to present a psychological phenomenon to help explain how the situation above unfolded. How could the pundits make decisions that were counter to the preponderance of evidence available to them? Can we learn how to improve decision making when it comes to using customer feedback data to improve the customer experience?

Confirmation Bias and Decision Making

Confirmation bias is a psychological phenomenon where people tend to favor information that confirms or supports their existing beliefs and ignores or discounts information that contradicts their beliefs.

Here are three different forms of confirmation bias with simple guidelines to help you minimize their impact on decision making. These guidelines are not meant to be comprehensive. Look at them as a starting point to help you think more critically about how you make decisions using customer data.

- **People tend to seek out information that supports their beliefs or hypotheses.** In our example, the pundits handpicked specific poll results to make/ support their predictions. What can you do? Specifically look for data to refute your beliefs. If you believe product quality is more important than service quality in predicting customer loyalty, be sure to collect evidence about the relative impact of service quality (compared to product quality).

- **Peopletendtorememberinformation that supports their position and not remember information that does not support their position.** Don't rely on your memory. When making decisions based on any kind of data, cite the specific reports/studies in which those data appear. Referencing your information source can help other people verify the information and help them understand your decision and how you arrived at it. If they arrive at a different conclusion than you, understand the source of the difference (data quality? different metrics? different analysis?).

- **People tend to interpret information in a way that supports their opinion.** There are a few things you can do to minimize the impact of confirmation bias. First, use inferential statistics to separate real, systematic, meaningful variance in the data from random noise. If you are using a graph to communicate a result, place a verbal description of the interpretation next to the graph. A clear description ensures that the graph has little room for misinterpretation. Also, let multiple people interpret the information contained in customer reports. People from different perspectives (e.g., IT vs. Marketing) might provide highly different (and revealing) interpretations of the same data.

Making Decisions

Once you start using data to drive your decisions, you need to understand how to best use those data. Next, I will discuss how understanding sampling error can help you make better decisions. I will begin by discussing the difference between samples and populations.

Samples and Populations

One thing that you need to know about statistics is the notion of sampling error. Sampling error reflects the difference of the sample of data from the population of data from which that sample was drawn. When we make conclusions about the population based on the smaller sample, we are making inferences. For example, if you are interested in understanding the satisfaction of your entire customer base, you measure the satisfaction of only a random sample of the entire population of customers.

We rarely (never) have access to the entire population of customers' perceptions of their experience with us. Instead, we rely on measuring a sample of customers to make conclusions about all of our customers. The use of statistics helps us understand if the observations we see in your customer feedback results (a sample) likely reflect what we would see for all of your customers (a population).

Any field that deals with using samples of data is impacted by sampling error. Medical researchers rely on the use of a sample of patients to study the effect of a treatment on disease. Polling organizations make nationwide predictions about outcomes of elections based on the responses of only 1000 respondents.

Sampling Error and the Need for Inferential Statistics

Inferential statistics is a set of procedures applied to a sample of data in order to determine how likely it reflects reality (the entire population). Because your sample-based findings are likely different than what you would find using the entire population, applying some statistical rigor to your sample helps you determine if what you see in the sample is what is actually occurring in the population; as such, the generalizations you make about the population need to be tempered using inferential statistics.

When Decision-Making Goes Wrong: Tampering with your Business Processes

Used in quality improvement circles, the term,

"tampering," refers to the process of adjusting a business process on the basis of results that are simply expected due to random errors. Putting data interpretation in the hands of people who do not appreciate the notion of sampling error can result in tampering of business processes. As a real example of tampering, I had the experience where an employee created a customer satisfaction trend line covering several quarters. The employee was implementing operational changes based on the fact that the trend line showed a drop in customer satisfaction in the current quarter. When pressed, the employee told me that each data point on the graph was based on a sample size of five (5!) respondents. Applying inferential statistics to the data, I found that the differences across the quarters were not based on real differences, but due, instead, to sampling error. Because of the small sample size, the observed differences across time were essentially noise. Making any changes to the business processes based on these results was simply not warranted.

Big Data Tools will not Create Data Scientists

There has been much talk about how new big data software solutions will help create an army of data scientists to help companies uncover insights in their data. I view these big data software solutions primarily as a way to help people visualize their data. Yes, visualization of your data is important, but, to be of value in helping you make the right decisions for your business, you need to know if the findings you observe in your data are meaningful and real. You can only accomplish this seemingly magical feat of data interpretation by applying inferential statistics to your data.

Inferential statistics allows you to apply some mathematical rigor to your data that go well beyond merely looking at data and applying the inter-ocular test (aka eyeballing the data). To be of value, data scientists in the area of customer experience management need a solid foundation of inferential statistics and an understanding of sampling error. Only then, can data scientists help their company distinguish signal (e.g., real differences) from the noise (e.g., random error).

Summary

My good friend and colleague, Stephen King (CEO of TCELab) put it well when describing the problem of not using data in decision-making: "In the absence of data, everyone is right." We tend to seek out information that supports our beliefs and disregard information that does not. This confirmation bias negatively impacts decisions by limiting what data we seek out and ignore and how we use those data. To minimize the impact of confirmation bias, act like a scientist. Test competing theories, cite your evidence and apply statistical rigor to your data.

As I will discuss next, using Big Data integration

principles to organize your disparate business data is one way to improve the quality of decision-making. Data integration around your customers facilitates the use of different metrics to track performance and improves hypothesis testing using different customer metrics across disparate data sources, improving how you make decisions that will ultimately help you make the right business decisions.

Section 3: Business Integration

"Above all else, show the data."

Edward Tufte

Senior executives of loyalty leading companies have customers at the heart of their business. They include customers as part of their corporate strategy and put governance plans in place to help guide proper use of business data, including customer data. Putting these activities in practice requires the integration of customer feedback into the businesses' processes.

This section of the book provides best practices that loyalty leaders adopt with respect to integrating CEM program elements into their business processes. The integration of different business processes with customer feedback requires the integration of different **sources of data**. Companies are adopting Big Data tools and principles to examine these different data sources, and loyalty leading companies maximize the value of their different data sources by linking them to customer feedback.

Chapter 6:
Best Practices
in Business
Integration

*"The unlike is joined together, and from differences
results the most beautiful harmony."*

Heraclitus

The area of Business Integration addresses the extent
to which the organization embeds elements of the CEM
program (including processes and data) into other
business operations and processes.

A customer-centric company is one that integrates
the program across all levels of the organization, from top
management to front-line employees. The integration can
occur in a variety of forms, from regular companywide
communications of the program's goals and processes to
dissemination of the results. Executives review customer
feedback metrics in their quarterly meetings. Account
managers use customer feedback as a regular part of
their account planning process. Call center agents draw
upon the caller's customer experience history to better

manage the transaction.

The advent of technological advancements (CRM systems, Internet) has greatly impacted the extent to which CEM programs can be integrated into business processes. Loyalty leading companies incorporate the CEM program into their CRM system and, consequently, are able to use both objective data (sales/service history) and attitudinal data (satisfaction) to get a comprehensive picture of the quality of the customer relationship.

For the customer-centric company, CEM programs play an important role in the management of the business. The integration of customer feedback into the business operations keeps the customers' needs in the fore of the management and front-line employees' mind. A list of best practices in Business Integration is located in Table 6.1.

Best Practices	The specifics...
6. Present customer feedback metrics in executive dashboards	Build and use summary scores (aggregate of several measures into fewer metrics) to track performance attributes for entire company and business units. Summary scores help communicate the general health of the customer relationship at a macro level (great for executive reporting).
7. Integrate the customer feedback program into business processes and technology	Use customer feedback metrics in meetings with your customers (B2B, account management). Use customer success stories to help develop marketing and sales materials. Integrate customer feedback metrics into your company CRM system to facilitate employees' access to customer feedback metrics.
8. Communicate all areas of the customer feedback program (e.g., process and goals) to the entire company	Develop a customer feedback portal on company intranet site to house all content related to customer feedback programs, including data collection methods, research results, satisfaction/loyalty trends, and customer success stories. Include information about the customer feedback program in employee training.
9. Integrate the resolution of customer issues into the company's Customer Relationship Management system	Develop a closed-loop process of problem notification to resolution. This can be facilitated by housing customer feedback metrics in the CRM system. Employ the power of the Web to immediately notify employees, typically account managers, of "at-risk" customers who respond negatively to specified survey questions.

Table 6.1. Best Practices in Business Integration

Chapter 7: Big Data in Customer Experience Management

"It's not information overload. It's filter failure."

Clay Shirky

Businesses today are relying on Big Data to gain a competitive advantage. The concept of Big Data is a broad one and I consider it an amalgamation of different areas that help us try to get a handle on, insight from and use out of data. Pat Gelsinger, President and COO of EMC, in an article in The Wall Street Journal said that Big Data refers to the idea that companies can extract value from collecting, processing and analyzing vast quantities of data. Businesses that can get a better handle on these data will be more likely to outperform their competitors who do not.

When describing Big Data, people typically refer to three characteristics of the data: 1) **Volume**: the amount of data being collected is massive; consider that 90 percent of all data in the world today has been in the last two years; 2) **Velocity**: the speed ̲ ̲ ̲ ̲ ̲ ̲ ̲ data are being generated/collected is very fast and needs to be analyzed as it comes in to identify fraud; and **Variety**: the different types of data like structured and unstructured data (e.g., images, videos and text from call center conversations). Recently introduced by IBM, **Veracity** describes an important fourth characteristic of data. To be of use to business, data must reflect reality (e.g., accurate, valid) and be trusted by the users.

Three Big Data Approaches

Brian Gentile, CEO of Jaspersoft, argues for a solution-oriented approach to understanding the value of Big Data. Before selecting a vendor, you first need to understand the problem you are trying solve. Keep in mind that Big Data is not just about analyzing data quickly; it is about analyzing data intelligently, perhaps with some theory-driven analyses. Gentile's three Big Data approaches include:

- **Interactive Exploration**: For discovering real-time patterns from your data as they emerge

- **Direct Batch Reporting**: For summarizing data into pre-built, scheduled (e.g., daily, weekly) reports

- **Batch ETL (extract-transform-load)**: For analyzing historical trends or linking disparate data sources based upon pre-defined questions. Sometimes called data federation, this approach involves pulling metrics from different data sources for purposes of understanding how all the metrics are related (in a correlation sense) to each other.

So, be sure to understand that Big Data is not just about *quick analysis* of your data. It is also about *integration* of different sources of data.

Disparate Sources of Business Data

Businesses have many different sources of data, each self-contained and built, if not for a singular purpose, at least to address problems in a specific business area. These data reside in four different data silos:

- **Operational:** Operational data contain objective metrics that measure the quality of the business processes and can come from a variety of sources. Hardware providers use sensors to monitor the quality of their implementations. Customer Relationship Management (CRM) systems track the quality of call center interactions (e.g., call length, response time).

- **Financial:** Financial data contain objective metrics that measure the quality of the financial health of the company and are typically housed in the company's financial reporting system.

- **Constituency (includes employees, partners):** Constituency data contain both attitudinal metrics as well as more objective metrics about specific constituents. Human Resources department has access to a variety of different types of data, ranging from employees' performance histories and completed training courses to survey results and salaries. Partner programs track partner information, including attitudes, financial investments, and sales growth.

- **Customer:** Customer data contain attitudinal metrics. Large enterprises rely on their Enterprise Feedback Management systems to capture and analyze data from such sources as surveys, social media and online communities.

Data Integration is Key to Extracting Value

Data integration is a difficult problem. Within a given company, data are housed in different systems. HR has their own system for tracking employee resources. The call center tracks data on their CRM system. Finance tracks their data on yet a different system. What approach can companies take to integrate all their data? In an interview on readwrite.com, Anjul Bhambhri, VP for Big Data for IBM, talked about how business can solve their Big Data integration problem with respect to data silos:

> "My response and suggestion - and we've actually done it with clients - has been that, you leave the data where it is. You're not going to start moving that around. You're not going to break those applications. You're not going to just rewrite those applications... just to solve this problem. Really, data federation and information integration is the way to go. Data is going to reside where it is."
>
> Anjul Bhambhri, VP for Big Data, IBM

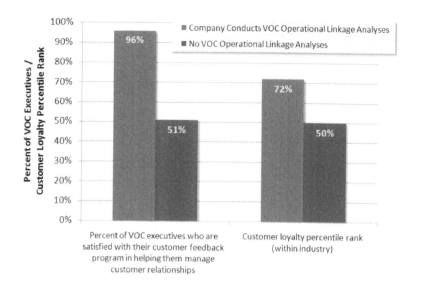

Figure 7.1. Companies who integrate operational data with their customer feedback get the insights that drive customer loyalty.

The problem of Big Data for businesses is one of applying appropriate data federation and analytic techniques to these disparate data sources to extract usable insight. I believe a useful way to approach this data problem rests with a customer-centric approach of data integration and analysis.

Data integration played a crucial role in the success of you CEM program (see Figure 7.1). Loyalty leading companies, compared to their loyalty lagging counterparts, integrated different sources of business data (e.g., operational, financial, constituency) with their customer feedback data. By linking disparate data sources to their customer feedback data, companies gain insight about what is important to the customers.

CEM programs can be data intensive, generating millions of data points about their customers' attitudes, online behaviors, and even their interactions with a given employee, just to name a few. The source of data in most CEM programs, not surprisingly, is customer feedback data. Businesses gain customer insight primarily by collecting and analyzing customer feedback data from different sources, including customer feedback surveys, social media sites, branded online communities and emails. Using customer feedback data, companies identify the customer experiences that are closely linked to customer loyalty and use that information to allocate resources to improve those customer experiences, and, consequently, increase customer loyalty.

Linkage Analysis

Integrating different business metrics to understand how they relate to each other is sometimes referred to as the process of Business Linkage Analysis. How you integrate/link your different metrics depends on the problem you are trying to solve or the question you are trying to answer.

For example, here are three popular questions that can be answered using linkage analysis of disparate data sources.

- What is the $ value of improving customer satisfaction / loyalty?

- Which call center metrics have the biggest impact on customer satisfaction/loyalty?

- Which employee/partner factors have the biggest impact on customer satisfaction/ loyalty?

Each question requires different datasets, merged at the right level for the appropriate analysis.

Integrating your Business Data

Even though many different data sources can be integrated in different ways, I refer to the overarching approach to business data integration as a "customer-centric" approach. This integration approach is one of organizing the data to gain insight about the causes and consequences of customer satisfaction / sentiment / loyalty.

Depending on the question you are trying to answer, you will use a combination of different sources of data. For example, when dealing with questions around financial metrics, you can integrate those with customer feedback at the relationship level via relationship surveys and social media sources. For operational or constituency-related question, you will need to consider other data sources and integration level (e.g., link data at transaction level instead of customer level).

You will need to apply appropriate data federation and aggregation processes to build specific data sets for statistical analyses interpretation for each question. For example, studying the impact of employee satisfaction on customer satisfaction requires a different data set than when studying the impact of call center metrics on customer satisfaction.

How Big Data can Advance Customer Experience Management

Customer feedback is just one type of data that needs to be analyzed and managed. By integrating different business data silos, businesses can more fully understand how other business metrics can impact or be impacted by customer satisfaction and loyalty. The impact that Big Data integration will have in CEM falls in three related areas: 1) Answering bigger questions about customers; 2) Building companies around the customers; 3) Predict real customer behaviors.

1. Answer Bigger Questions about Customers

Businesses gain customer insight primarily by analyzing customer feedback data with little or no regard for other data sources. By linking disparate data sources to their customer feedback data, companies gain insight about their customers that they could not achieve by looking at their customer feedback data alone.

Businesses can now ask, and, more importantly, answer these types of questions.

- Where do we **set operational goals** in our call centers (e.g., number of handoffs, length of wait time) to ensure we maximize customer satisfaction?

- How many hours of training do **employees need** to ensure they can satisfy their customers?

- Which **call center metrics are the key determinants of customer satisfaction** with the call center experience?

- Where do we need to invest in our **employee relationship** (e.g., across the employee experience touch points) to ensure they deliver a great customer experience?

- Do customers who report higher loyalty **spend** more than customers who report lower levels of loyalty?

Companies who integrate their business data to

understand the correlates of customer satisfaction and loyalty can better answer these questions and, consequently, have a much better advantage of effectively allocating their resources in areas that they know will help improve the customer experience and maximize customer loyalty and business growth.

2. Build your Company around the Customer

Big Data principles can help you create a customer-centric culture. By integrating different sources of business data and uncovering insights about a variety of different metrics, you build interest across different organizations in understanding what is important to the customers. The integration of different business data would necessarily involve key stakeholders from each organization, and the mere act of integration would be a catalyst for further cross-organizational discussions about the customer. Applying a customer-centric data federation and aggregation approach to business data integration helps senior leaders understand how their organization (and its metrics) impacts the customer.

Additionally, the results of customer research become more applicable to other organizations or departments when their data are used. Expanding the use of customer data to other departments (e.g., HR, Call Center, and Marketing) helps the entire company improve processes that are important to the customer. Here are some examples of how companies are using this type of research to build a customer-centric culture.

- Identifying and building customer-centric operational metrics for executive dashboards

- Removing the noise from executive reports by including only customer-centric business metrics (known to be predictive of customer satisfaction and loyalty)

- Integrating customer feedback into operational systems (CRM) so front-line employees understand the interactions *and* attitudes of their customers

- Conducting in-depth customer research using all business data to continually uncover customer insights and gain a competitive advantage

Big Data technologies and processes can go a long way in helping you support your CEM program. By taking a customer-centric approach to your Big Data, you will be able to literally build the company (its data) around the customer.

3. Predict Real Customer Behaviors

Despite the existence of objective measures of customer loyalty (e.g., customer renews contract, recommends you, buys more), CEM programs rely on customer surveys as a way to assess customer loyalty. Measures of customer loyalty typically take the form of questions that ask the customer to indicate his or her **likelihood of engaging in specific types of behaviors**, those deemed important to the company/brand.

Companies often rely on self-report measures as their only measure of customer loyalty. While these loyalty metrics do provide reliable, valid and useful information, you are always interested in what customers really do. By linking up financial data and customer feedback data, you would be able to understand how the customer experience impacts **real customer loyalty behavior using objective metrics**, like purchase amount, products purchased, products liked, products shared and renewed contract.

End-of-quarter financial reports include customer loyalty metrics (e.g., churn rates, ARPU, repurchase rates) with no information about the factors that might impact those numbers. Traditionally analyzed at the end of the quarter as standalone metrics, these objective loyalty metrics provide no insight about how to improve them. Linking satisfaction with the customer experience to these objective loyalty measures, however, lets you build predictive models to help you understand the reasons behind your financial metrics.

Summary

The era of Big Data is upon us and the Big Data problem for business is one of linking up their disparate data silos with customer feedback data in order to identify the correlates of customer satisfaction and loyalty. A major hurdle in solving this problem involves applying appropriate **data federation and aggregation** methods across the different data silos. This data federation process results in usable datasets with the right metrics culled from different data sources to answer specific questions or hypotheses. Once the metrics are pulled from their respective data sources, businesses can apply statistical modeling to answer important questions about the causes of customer satisfaction and loyalty.

Big Data principles play a major role in CEM programs. Integrating other sources of business data with your customer feedback data can help you extract much more value from each of your data sources. By linking up these data sources, you will be able to ask and answer bigger customer experience questions, embed the importance of the customer across different organizations / departments and provide the use of both subjective and objective metrics of customer loyalty.

Chapter 8: Analyzing Business Data Using a Customer-Centric Approach

"One of the issues of social networking silos is that they have the data and I don't."

Tim Berners-Lee

Customer experience management professionals are asked to demonstrate the value of their CEM programs. They are asked: Does the program measure attitudes that are related to real customer behavior? How do we set operational goals to ensure we maximize customer satisfaction? Are the customer feedback metrics predictive of our future financial performance and business growth? Do customers who report higher loyalty spend more than customers who report lower levels of loyalty? To answer these questions, companies look to a process called business linkage analysis.

Business Linkage Analysis is the process of

combining different sources of data (e.g., customer, employee, partner, financial, and operational) to uncover important relationships among important variables (e.g., call handle time and customer satisfaction). For our context, linkage analysis will refer to the linking of other data sources to customer feedback metrics (e.g., customer satisfaction, customer loyalty).

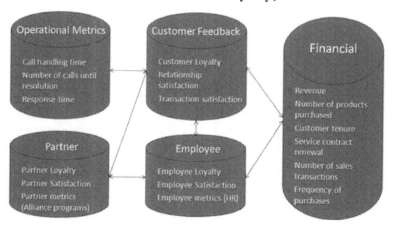

Figure 8.1. Linking Disparate Business Data Sources Leads to Insight

Linkage analyses appear to have a positive impact on customer loyalty by providing executives the insights they need to manage customer relationships. These insights give loyalty leaders an advantage over loyalty laggards. Loyalty leaders apply linkage analyses results in a variety of ways to build a more customer-centric company: Determine the ROI of different improvement efforts, create customer-centric operational metrics (important to customers) and set employee training standards to ensure they deliver a great customer experience, to name a few.

Linkage Analysis: A Data Management and Analysis Problem

You can think of linkage analysis as a two-step process: 1) organizing two disparate data sources into one coherent dataset and 2) conducting analyses on that aggregated dataset. The primary hurdle in any linkage analysis is organizing the data in an appropriate way where the resulting linked dataset make logical sense for our analyses. Therefore, data management and statistical skills are essential in conducting a linkage analysis study.

Once the data are organized, the researcher is able to conduct nearly any kind of statistical analyses he/she want (e.g., Regression, ANOVA, Multivariate), as long as it makes sense given the types of variables (e.g., nominal, interval) you are using.

Types of Linkage Analyses

In business, linkage analyses are conducted using the following types of data:

- Customer Feedback

- Financial

- Operational

- Employee

- Partner

Even though I discuss these data sources as if they are distinct, separate sources of data, it is important to note that some companies have some of these data sources housed in one dataset (e.g., call center system can house transaction details including operational metrics and customer satisfaction with that transaction). While this is an advantage, these companies still need to ensure their data are organized together in an appropriate way to support the goals of predictive modeling.

With these data sources, we can conduct three general types of linkage analyses:

- **Financial**: Linking customer feedback to financial metrics

- **Operational**: Linking customer feedback to operational metrics

- **Constituency**: Linking customer feedback to employee and partner variables

Before we go further, I need to make an important distinction between two different types of customer feedback sources: 1) relationship-based and 2) transaction-based. In relationship-based feedback, customer ratings (data) reflect their overall experience

with and loyalty towards the compa
based feedback, customer ratings
experience with a specific event
distinction is necessary because difie
analyses require different types of customer feedbac
data (See Figure 8.2). Relationship-based customer feedback is needed to conduct financial linkage analyses and transaction-based customer feedback is needed to conduct operational linkage analyses.

Customer Feedback Data Sources

Business Data Sources	Relationship Survey (satisfaction/loyalty to company)	Transactional Survey (satisfaction with specific transaction/interaction)	Social Media/ Communities (sentiment / shares / likes)
Financial (revenue, number of sales)	• Link data at customer level • Quality of the relationship (sat, loyalty) impacts financial metrics	N/A	• Link data at customer level • Quality of relationship (sentiment / likes / shares) impacts financial metrics
Operational (call handling, response time)	N/A	• Link data at transaction level • Operational metrics impact quality of the transaction	• Link data at transaction level • Operational metrics impact sentiment / likes/ shares
Constituency (employee / partner feedback)	• Link data at constituency level • Constituency satisfaction impacts customer satisfaction with overall relationship	• Link data at constituency level • Constituency satisfaction impacts customer satisfaction with interaction	• Link data at constituency level • Constituency satisfaction impacts customer sentiment / likes / shares

Figure 8.2. Common Types of Linkages among Disparate Data Sources

Summary

Business linkage analysis is the process of combining

rent sources of data to uncover important insights bout the causes and consequence of customer satisfaction and loyalty. For CEM programs, linkage analyses fall into three general types: financial, operational, and constituency. Each of these types of linkage analyses provides useful insight that can help senior executives better manage customer relationships and improve business growth. I will provide examples of each type of linkage analyses in the following chapters.

Chapter 9: Linking Financial and Customer Metrics

"In the long run managements stressing accounting appearance over economic substance usually achieve little of either."

Warren Buffett

For financial linkage analysis, we are interested in understanding the relationship between customer feedback metrics and financial business outcomes. Demonstrating the statistical relationship between customer feedback metrics and financial business outcomes is useful for three reasons:

- **Strengthen business case for your CEM program:** Demonstrating your customer feedback metrics predict future bottom line metrics shows executives that tracking/measuring customer satisfaction/ loyalty has some monetary value (e.g., increase in ratings is followed by increase in revenue). Senior executives' support of the CEM program is paramount to its success, and demonstrating the monetary value of your program goes a long way in establishing the value of the CEM program. A customer-financial linkage study can quickly illustrate the reasons why you have a CEM program and the important business outcomes it predicts.

- **Identify drivers of real customer behaviors:** In typical CEM programs, we measure customer loyalty via survey questions that let customers indicate their future loyalty behaviors (recommend, buy again, not churn). Using linkage analysis, we can use real customer loyalty behaviors in our analysis. Taking this approach, we can understand drivers of real customer behaviors (number of products purchased, sales amount).

- **Determine ROI for customer experience improvement solutions:** Improving customer loyalty may require significant investment to improve the customer experience. Financial linkage analysis can help you understand the expected increases in financial performance given a specific improvement in customer satisfaction.

Financial and Customer Feedback Metrics

I use the term, "financial metrics," to include various types of business outcomes that can be used in linkage analyses. These metrics include:

- Customer tenure

- Customer defection rate

- Number of new customers

- Revenue

- Service contract renewal

- Number of sales transactions

- Number of products purchased

- Frequency of purchases

It is important to note that the specific details of conducting linkage analyses may vary slightly for different metrics; the level at which the financial metric can be summarized (by geography, by time, by customer) reflects the level at which the datasets need to be merged. If you are able to track revenue for each customer, you can associate the customer feedback metric with each customer's revenue. On the other hand, if you are able to track defection rate at the group level, you can associate the customer feedback metric with each group's defection rate. The key here is to ensure the level of analysis (e.g., customer, geography, time-level) makes sense given the level of measurement of your financial metric.

In financial linkage studies, we use customer feedback metrics from a relationship-based survey where responses indicate general levels of satisfaction and loyalty toward the company. Additionally, it is important to note that these customer feedback metrics need to be from respondents who are responsible for, or have an influence in, purchasing decisions. Customer feedback metrics from relationship-based surveys could include loyalty questions/indices or satisfaction with business attributes (customer experience).

Linking Financial Metrics to Customer Metrics

Once we have these two sources of business data, we organize the data so that each customer (or group or time period) has a score on the financial metric and the customer feedback metric. The example in Figure 9.1 represents the linkage at the customer level (For a B2B example, the merging can occur at the Account level). For each customer (account), we have two pieces of information, customer feedback (x) and a business outcome (y).

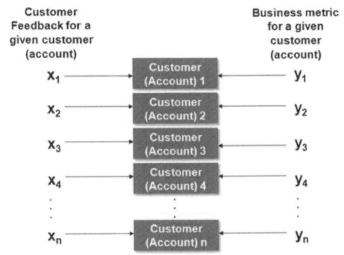

x_n represents the customer feedback for customer (account) n.
y_n represents the business metric for customer (account) n.

Figure 9.1. Data model for financial linkage analysis

Loyalty metrics are forward looking (e.g., likelihood to behave in certain positive ways in the future). As such, financial linkage analysis needs to involve loyalty metrics measured at one time (Time 1) and financial metrics measured at a later time (Time 2). The nature of the regular sales cycle will have an impact on loyalty behaviors, so careful thought needs to be given to the length between the two time periods.

Results

The output of the analyses will illustrate the relationship between customer satisfaction/loyalty and business outcomes. When presenting the results of the analysis, I like to illustrate the relationship in graphical form. Below are two figures that show the relationship between customer satisfaction/loyalty metrics and important business outcomes.

Figure 9.2. Relationship between Customer Loyalty and Maintenance Renewals

Figure 9.2 illustrates the relationship between customer loyalty and downsizes in maintenance renewals. Accounts who reported they were disloyal in Q1 2010 are more likely to result in downsizes in maintenance renewals for Q4 2010 compared to accounts who reported they were loyal in Q1 2010.Figure 9.3 illustrates the relationship between customer satisfaction with technical account managers (TAMs) and revenue. Accounts that are more satisfied with Technical Account Management (TAM) performance in Q1 2010 have significantly higher revenue from maintenance renewals in Q4 2010 compared to account that are dissatisfied with TAM performance in Q1 2010.

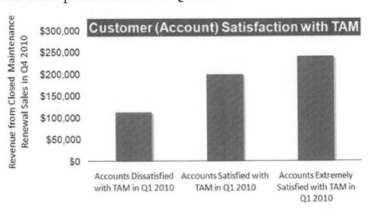

Figure 9.3. Relationship between Satisfaction with Technical Account Manager (TAM) and Revenue

Using the results of these analyses, senior executives were able to estimate the increased revenue they would expect (additional revenue and saved revenue) given improvements in customer satisfaction.

Summary

Financial linkage analysis helps show the consequences of customer satisfaction and loyalty and demonstrate the monetary value of the customer metrics. In my examples, the linkage analyses showed us that customer feedback metrics (customer satisfaction with tech support and satisfaction with technical account managers) were, in fact, predictive of future business metrics (maintenance renewals and revenue, respectively).

Chapter 10: Linking Operational and Customer Metrics

"Not everything that can be counted counts, and not everything that counts can be counted."

Albert Einstein

For operational linkage analysis, we are interested in understanding the relationship between customer feedback metrics and operational metrics. Demonstrating the statistical relationship between customer feedback metrics and operational metrics is useful for three reasons:

- **Build/Identify customer-centric business metrics:** Operational linkage analysis helps you identify / create key operational metrics that are statistically linked to customer satisfaction.

- **Manage customer relationships using objective operational metrics:** You can manage the customer relationship using clear operational metrics. Linkage analysis will help in setting appropriate operational performance goals (using operational metrics) that ensure customers will be satisfied.

- **Reward employee behavior that will drive customer satisfaction:** Because of their reliability and specificity, operational metrics are good candidates for use in goal setting and employee incentive programs. Rewarding employee performance based on customer-centric operational metrics ensures employees understand what's important to the customers.

Next, I will illustrate how linkage analysis is conducted using operational and customer feedback metrics.

Operational and Customer Feedback Metrics

There are many types of operational metrics used to assess the quality of support and call centers. These metrics include:

- First Call Resolution (FCR) / Number of calls until resolution

- Call handling time

- Response time

- Abandon rate

- Adherence & Shrinkage

- Average talk time

- Average speed of answer (ASA)

In operational linkage studies, we use customer feedback metrics from a transaction-based survey where responses are associated with a specific transaction (typically, in a call-center environment) and reflect satisfaction with that specific transaction (or satisfaction with other components of the transaction - knowledge of call center rep). So, for any given transaction, we have two kinds of information, 1) the operational metrics surrounding that transaction and 2) customer's satisfaction with that transaction.

Linking Operational Metrics to Customer Metrics

Once we have these two sources of business data, we organize the data so that each transaction (or group or time period) has a score on the operational metric and the customer feedback metric. The example in Figure 10.1 represents the linkage at the transaction level. For each transaction (interaction), we have two pieces of information, operational metric (x) and customer feedback (y).

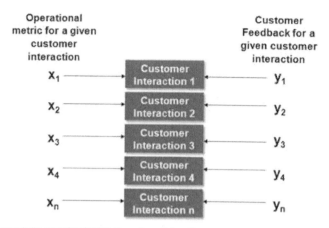

X$_n$ represents the operational metric for customer interaction n.
y$_n$ represents the customer feedback for customer interaction n.

Figure 10.1. Data Model for Operational Linkage Analysis

Results

The output of the analyses will illustrate the relationship between operational metrics and customer satisfaction. Below are two figures that show the relationship between different operational metrics and customer satisfaction.

Figure 10.2 illustrates the relationship between number of calls to resolve the service request (SR) and customer satisfaction with that SR. We found that SRs that required more calls from the customer resulted in lower levels of satisfaction with SRs compared to SRs that required fewer calls from the customer. Specifically, customers were satisfied until they had to call four times. As a result, senior executives were able to implement a performance standard for SR resolutions (Resolve SRs within 3 telephone calls).

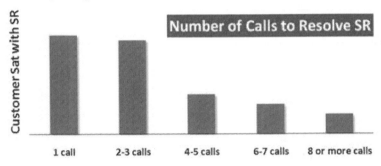

Figure 10.2. Number of calls to resolve Service Request (SR) is related to customer satisfaction with that SR

Figure 10.3 illustrates the relationship of two operational metrics (initial response time and total time to resolve SR) with customer satisfaction with SRs.

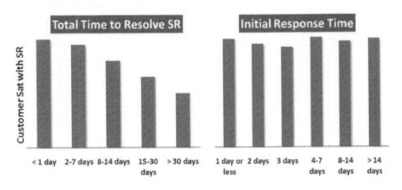

Figure 10.3. Linkage analysis used to identify which operational metrics are important to customers

As you can see in the figure, initial response time had no impact on customer satisfaction; customers were just as satisfied with SRs that had a long initial response time as they were with SRs that had a shorter initial response time. On the other hand, total time to resolve the SR had a large impact on customer satisfaction with the SR. Customers were significantly more satisfied with SRs that were resolved within one week compared to SRs that took longer to resolve. From these results, it appears that resolution speed is much more important than initial response time.

Using the results of these analyses, senior executives were able to identify the call center operational metrics that impact customer satisfaction. As a result, senior executives wanted to understand how other operational metrics impacted customer satisfaction with the SR process in order to build a performance dashboard where only the important, customer-centric, operational metrics are displayed and tracked.

Summary

Operational linkage analysis helps show the causes of customer satisfaction. In my examples, the linkage analyses showed us that not all operational metrics are created equal. Companies turn to operational linkage analysis to identify those objective, measurable aspects of the transaction that drive customer satisfaction. Once identified, operational metrics can be used to manage customer relationships by incentivizing employees using operational metrics that matter to the customer.

Chapter 11: Linking Constituency and Customer Metrics

"The essence of competitiveness is liberated when we make people believe that what they think and do is important - and then get out of their way while they do it."

Jack Welch

The service profit chain depicted in Figure 11.1 (I added a partner variable and expanded customer loyalty) supports the belief that employee and partner management is key to ensuring customer loyalty and business growth. Constituency linkage analysis allows us to better understand how employees and partner relationships impact the health of the customer relationships.

Employee, Partner, and Customer Loyalty Drive Business Results

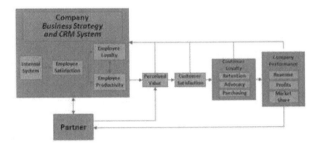

Based on the book, The Service Profit Chain: How leading Companies Link Profit and Growth to Loyalty, Satisfaction and Value (Heskett, Sasser & Schlesinger, 1997)

Figure 11.1. Service Delivery Model Highlights the Impact of Employees and Partners on Customer Loyalty and Business Growth

As this model illustrates, business growth is dependent on customer loyalty, which is, in turn impacted by employee satisfaction/loyalty and partner satisfaction/loyalty. Demonstrating the statistical relationship between customer feedback metrics and constituency metrics is useful for three related reasons:

- **Understand the impact of employee and partner experience on the customer experience:** Constituency linkage analysis helps you identify which employee/partner metrics are statistically linked to customer satisfaction.

- **Improve the health of the customer relationship by improving the health of the employee and partner relationship.** Managing customer relationships does not occur in a vacuum. Understanding how these other constituencies impact customer satisfaction and loyalty helps senior executives allocate the right resources across the entire ecosystem to drive business growth. Companies need to manage all different types of relationships (employee, partner, customer); a problem in one could impact the rest.

- **Help build a customer centric culture.** Constituency linkage results can help executives communicate the importance of the entire ecosystem in driving customer satisfaction and loyalty. Evangelizing how important the employees and partners are in helping ensure customers receive a great customer experience can be supported with these linkage studies.

Constituency and Customer Feedback Metrics

There are many types of constituency metrics that are commonly measured. Any metric tracked by human resources (HR) are candidates for employee metrics that we can use in linkage analysis. Additionally, many partner metrics (e.g., certification status, revenue) are candidates for linkage analysis. Some example metrics used in constituency linkage analysis include:

- Satisfaction metrics (employee sat and partner sat)

- Loyalty metrics (employee loyalty and partner loyalty)

- Employee training metrics

- Partner certification status

In constituency linkage studies, we can use customer feedback metrics from either a relationship-based or a transaction-based survey, as long as customer metrics can be aggregated at the appropriate unit of analysis (typically at the employee or partner level). So, for any given constituency, we can have two kinds of information, 1) their employee/partner metric (sat, loyalty, HR) and 2) customer's satisfaction/loyalty metric.

Linking Constituency Metrics to Customer Metrics

Once we have these two sources of business data, we organize the data at the employee/partner level (each employee has a score on the constituency metric and a customer feedback metric (see Figure 11.2). Linking an employee metric to a given employee is straightforward.

There is a 1 to 1 ratio of employee to employee metric (Employee 1 has Employee 1 Metric; Employee 2 has Employee 2 Metric).

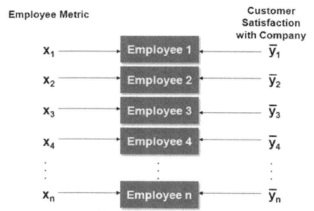

Analysis typically conducted for B2B customers where a given employee (sales representative, technical account manager, sales manager) is associated with a given customer (account)

x_n represents employee satisfaction score for Employee n.

$\bar{y}_n$ represents average customer satisfaction scores across survey respondents for Employee n.

Figure 11.2. Data Model for Constituency - Customer Linkage

Considering the customer feedback metric, a given employee could have more than one customer response associated to him/her. There is a 1-to-many ratio of employees to customer feedback responses. The customer metric for each employee, then, would be the average of the customer responses for that employee. In large B2B enterprise companies, a specific employee (Account Managers, Technical Account Managers, and

Consulting Services) can be assigned to specific Accounts. Therefore, each employee could have multiple customer feedback responses associated to him/her; the customer metric for this employee would be the average rating across all his/her responses. In a B2C environment, call center agents can be linked to several, specific customer interactions; each employee's customer metric would be the average rating across all his/her interactions. So, if an employee had customer satisfaction ratings from 10 customers, his customer metric would be the average of those 10 customers.

The bottom line is that employees/partners can have feedback from multiple customers. If you are able, obtaining all relevant customer data points for each employee/partner results in more reliable measures of employees' and partners' performance. The data model in Figure 11.2 represents the linkage at the employee level. For each employee, we have two pieces of information, constituency metric (x) and customer feedback (y - average over the different customers the employee served).

Results

The output of the analyses will illustrate the relationship between the constituency metrics and the customer metric. Below are three figures that show the relationship constituency metrics and customer metrics.

In an enterprise software company, the Technical Account Managers (TAMs) are responsible for implementing the software into the company's infrastructure. Figure 11.3 illustrates the results of a linkage study that examined how Technical Account Managers' attitudes toward the company impacts customers' satisfaction with the implementation. We found that TAMs that were highly satisfied with their company also had customers who were more satisfied with the TAM's implementation. It appears that, to ensure customers are satisfied with their implementation, the company needs to ensure the TAMs are satisfied.

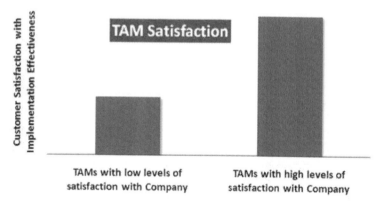

Figure 11.3. Employees who are satisfied deliver a better customer experience

Figure 11.4 illustrates the impact of training on customer satisfaction. Employing a linkage study, this company was able to link training metrics and customer satisfaction metrics for specific TAMs. The company was spending much money on employee training and wanted to determine its effectiveness on improving customer satisfaction. As you can see in Figure 11.4, TAMs who completed 4 or more courses had customers who were more satisfied with their performance than TAMs who completed 1-3 courses.

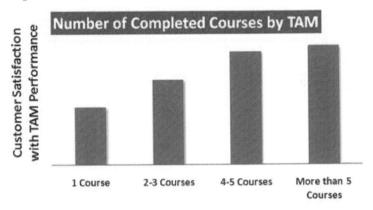

Figure 11.4. Employee training has a positive impact on customer satisfaction

In the same enterprise software company, business partners (system integrators) were used to help integrate the software into joint customers' accounts. To understand how partner relationships impact joint customer relationships, the company wanted to examine the linkage between partner and customer metrics. Because a given Account had only one system integrator, we could easily link partner metrics and customer metrics via partners (system integrators). Figure 11.5 illustrates this relationship. The company found that customers were much more satisfied with the implementation when the system integrator was also loyal to the company.

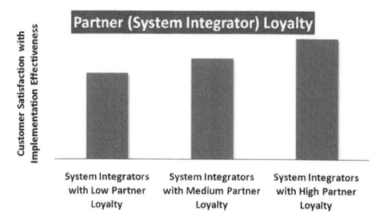

Figure 11.5. System integrators (partners) who are loyal to the company have customers who are satisfied with the implementation

The results of these analyses helped senior executives evangelize the importance of employees and partners in delivering great customer service. The senior executives were able to determine the value of employee training on customer satisfaction and set appropriate training goals that ensured customers were satisfied with the implementation of their solution. The partner-customer linkage study supported the need for a formal partner relationship program. The company implemented a more formal partner program in which partner survey results were used to improve partner satisfaction.

Section 4: Method and Reporting

"However beautiful the strategy, you should occasionally look at the results."

Winston Churchill

In the prior chapters, I focused primarily on managerial aspects around CEM programs that address how the company sets strategy, uses data and organizes the business (and its data) around the customer. Next, I turn to aspects of a CEM program that are more operational in nature and reflect more of a "how-to" guide into measuring customers' attitudes, reporting the data and applying analytics to gain a deeper insight into the causes of and consequences of customer satisfaction and loyalty.

In this section, I will show that measuring customer attitudes does not require many questions. I will present a Customer Loyalty Measurement Framework that will help you determine the types of loyalty metrics you need to track in your business and how to measure them. I will critique the popular NPS approach to measuring loyalty and identify some drawbacks to this measurement method. To help you avoid "net scores," I will demonstrate a better way to summarize your data that is both simple and meaningful.

Chapter 12: Best Practices in Method and Reporting

"If you do not know how to ask the right question, you discover nothing."

W. Edward Deming

Method

The method of your CEM program addresses the means by which the organization collects customer feedback data (See Figure 12.1). One popular method of gathering feedback is through a structured collection process like a survey that asks standardized questions about the customers' experience with the service/product/brand. Another data collection method is less structured and includes the use of social media sites and online brand communities where customers can communicate (e.g., "tweet") in a free-form format about their experience or seek support for a problem. All methods provide a rich source of data.

Figure 12.1. Structured surveys, social media and online brand communities provide methods for collecting customer feedback.

Loyalty leaders typically adopt a Web-based survey approach to collecting customer feedback across a variety of survey types (e.g., transactional, relationship, targeted). Web surveys facilitate the integration of the customer feedback into business processes and systems (e.g., CRM), thereby helping loyalty leading companies easily and quickly understand different customer constituencies.

Ensure your customer survey asks the right questions. Measuring the customer experience (CX) requires fewer questions than you think. It turns out that around 7 general CX questions will tell you just as much about what drives customer loyalty as 20-30 specific CX questions will (more on that later).

Customer metrics play a crucial role in understanding the health of the customer relationship. Don't go overboard on the customer metrics. As a general rule, select/use a few key customer metrics.

Loyalty leaders measure various components of customer loyalty that are designed for the company's specific needs. Rather than relying on one single measure of customer loyalty, loyalty leaders measure different types of loyalty (retention, advocacy and purchasing), gaining insight that helps them grow their business through new and existing customers (Hayes, 2011, Hayes, 2008a, 2008c; 2009; Keiningham, et al. 2007; Morgan & Rego, 2006).

In addition to measuring your own performance, assess your relative performance (compared to your competitors). Understanding your relative performance helps you identify your competitive dis/advantage and can help you improve your industry ranking.

Reporting

The quality of the CEM program does not stop at the collection of the customer feedback. Loyalty leaders know how to best analyze, summarize and present the customer feedback so the company is able to make useful business decisions.

Loyalty leaders apply the following two general loyalty management approaches using customer feedback: 1) micro approach and 2) macro approach. The micro approach is focused on addressing the concerns of a specific customer. The macro approach is focused on addressing systemic issues that impact large customer segments. Table 12.1 below summarizes these two general approaches.

Micro Approach	Macro Approach
1. Addresses special causes of disloyalty, one customer at a time	1. Addresses common causes of disloyalty across entire customer segments
2. Focus on special actions unique to the problem	2. Focus on process/system changes
3. Immediate implementation	3. Operational/Strategic changes
4. Customer-specific improvements	4. Organization-wide improvements

Table 12.1. Manage specific customers (Micro approach) and groups of customers (Macro approach)

As a general rule, reporting of the customer feedback results needs to be guided by the overarching company goals: improving customer loyalty. Loyalty leaders analyze the data to identify the reasons that cause customer loyalty. Once these causes are known, executives are armed with the knowledge on how to best maximize customer loyalty. A list of best practices for Method and Reporting is located in Table 12.2.

Best Practices	The specifics...
10. Use automated (e.g., Web) tools to collect and report customer feedback metrics	Web tools not only facilitate data collection, but with the ever-increasing adoption of a Web lifestyle, they are also becoming a necessity. Data collection via the Web is cost-effective, allows for quick integration with other data sources and speeds reporting of customer feedback.
11. Use different measures of customer loyalty	Selecting the right mix of customer loyalty questions will ensure you can grow your business through new and existing customers. Determine the important customer loyalty behaviors (retention, advocacy, purchasing) and measure them. Multiple questions improve reliability of the results (Cronbach, 1951; Nunnally, 1978).
12. Use multiple methods to collect customer feedback	Use a variety of sources of customer feedback to get comprehensive picture of the customer experience. Relationship surveys are effective at assessing general attitudes about the overall quality of the customer relationship. Transactional surveys are effective at assessing the quality of a specific interaction with the company. Social media sites and online brand communities offer another vehicle for customer feedback.
13. Present customer feedback program results throughout the company	Build a customer feedback portal on company's intranet site to house all information related to the customer feedback program. Use Web-based reporting tools for easy access by all employees, no matter where they are located in the world. Regularly publish customer research results in the company communiqué.
14. Incorporate customer contact management of the customer feedback program into the CRM system	Integration with existing customer information systems helps ensure the right customers are surveyed at the right time. This integration supports the linkage of survey results to specific Contact(s) within Accounts, helping you understand both attitudinal and behavioral measures of the health of your customer relationships.

Table 12.2. Best Practices in Method and Reporting

Statistical Analysis

The required step between collecting your data and reporting your data is statistical analysis. You can use a variety of statistical methods to extract insight from your data. Four general types of analyses that are useful in analyzing your customer data are presented below. For a fuller discussion of these methods, please see the book, Measuring Customer Satisfaction and Loyalty.

- **Correlational analysis (e.g., Pearson correlations, regression analysis):** This class of analyses helps us identify the linear relationship between customer satisfaction/loyalty metrics and other business metrics.

- **Factor analysis:** Generally, factor analysis is used when you have a large number of variables in your data set and would like to reduce the number down to a manageable size. By examining the relationship (e.g., correlation) among the original set of variables, a factor analysis groups similar variables together. Often used in scale construction, factor analysis helps you create indices from different survey questions. For example, 12 "service quality" questions might really represent only 2 different dimensions: service representative quality and technical solution quality.

- **Analysis of Variance (ANOVA):** Analysis of variance (ANOVA) is used to compare two or more groups. As the name of the analysis implies, ANOVA is a method of analyzing components of variance. This type of analysis helps us identify the potentially non-linear relationships between the customer satisfaction/loyalty metrics and other business metrics. For example, it is possible that increases in customer satisfaction/loyalty will not translate into improved business metrics until customer satisfaction/loyalty reaches a critical level.

- **Machine Learning:** Broadly speaking, machine learning is about designing algorithms for machines to optimize or improve results based on restrictions of the programmer. Machine learning, a type of artificial intelligence, uses existing or training data to make better predictions using new data. Machine learning programs detect patterns in data and adjust the program accordingly. For example, if you frequently do searches on Google for a specific topic and click on those links,

Google will present more advertisements to you that reflect that specific topic without human intervention.

Chapter 13: Four Criteria for your Customer Metric

"Once we know something, we find it hard to imagine what it was like not to know it."

Chip and Dan Heath

A successful customer experience management program requires the collection, synthesis, analysis and dissemination of different types of business metrics, including operational, financial, constituency and customer metrics. The quality of customer metrics necessarily impacts your understanding of how to best manage customer relationships to improve the customer experience, increase customer loyalty and grow your business. Using the wrong customer metrics could lead to sub-optimal decisions while using the right customer metrics can lead to good decisions that give you a competitive edge.

Customer Metrics

Customer metrics are **numerical scores or indices** that summarize customer feedback results.

They can be based on either customer average satisfaction rating with product qι ended customer comments (via sentiment analysιs). Additionally, customer ratings can be based on a **single item** or an **aggregated set of items** (averaging over a set of items to get a single score/metric).

Meaning of Customer Metrics

Customer metrics represent more than just numerical scores. Customer metrics have a deeper meaning, representing some underlying characteristic/ mental processes about your customers: their opinions and attitudes about and intentions toward your company or brand. Figure 13.1 depicts this relationship between the feedback tool (questions) and this overall score that we label as something. Gallup claims to measure customer engagement using 11 survey questions. Other practitioners have developed their unique metrics that assess underlying customer attitudes / intentions. The SERVQUAL method assesses several dimensions of service quality; the RAPID Loyalty approach measures three types of customer loyalty: retention, advocacy and purchasing. The Net Promoter Score® is yet another measure of customer loyalty.

Figure 13.1. Advocacy Loyalty Index (customer metric) measures extent to which customers will advocate/ feel positively toward your company (underlying construct) using three items/questions.

Customer Metrics are Necessary for Effective CEM Programs but not Frequently Used

Loyalty leading companies compared to their loyalty lagging counterparts, adopt specific customer feedback practices that require the use of customer metrics: sharing customer results throughout the company, including customer feedback in company/executive dashboards, compensating employees based on customer feedback, linking customer feedback to operational metrics, and identify improvement opportunities that maximize ROI.

Despite the usefulness of customer metrics, few businesses gather them. In a study examining the use of customer experience (CX) metrics, Bruce Temkin found that only about half (52%) of businesses collect and communicate customer experience (CX) metrics. Even fewer of them review CX metrics with cross-functional teams (39%), tie compensation to CX metrics (28%) or make trade-offs between financial and CX metrics (19%).

Evaluating Your Customer Metrics

As companies continue to grow their CEM programs and adopt best practices, they will rely more and more on the use of customer metrics. Whether you are developing your own in-house customer metric or using a proprietary customer metric, you need to be able to critically evaluate them to ensure they are meeting the needs of your CEM program. Here are four questions to ask about your customer metrics.

1. What is the definition of the customer metric?

Customer metrics need to be supported by a clear description of what it is measuring. Basically, the customer metric is defined the way that words are defined in the dictionary. They are non-ambiguous and straightforward. The definition, referred to as the constitutive definition, not only tells you what the customer metric is measuring, it also tells you what the customer metric is *not* measuring.

The complexity of the definition will match the complexity of the customer metric itself. Depending on the customer metric, definitions can reflect a narrow concept or a more complex concept. For single-item metrics, definitions are fairly narrow. For example, a customer metric based on the satisfaction rating of a single overall product quality question would have the following definition: "Satisfaction with product quality". For customer metrics that are made up of several items, a well-articulated definition is especially important. These customer metrics measure something more nuanced than single-item customer metrics.

2. How is the customer metric calculated?

Closely related to question 1, you need to convey precisely how the customer metric is calculated. Understanding how the customer metric is calculated requires understanding two things: 1) the specific items/questions in the customer metric; 2) how items/questions were combined to get to the final score. Knowing the specific items and how they are combined help define what the customer metric is measuring (operational definition). Any survey instructions and information about the rating scale (numerical and verbal anchors) need to be included.

3. What are the measurement properties of the customer metric?

Measurement properties refer to scientifically-derived indices that describe the quality of a customer metric. Applying the field of psychometrics and scientific measurement standards (see Standards for Educational and Psychological Testing), you can evaluate the quality of customer metrics. Analyzing existing customer feedback data, you are able to evaluate customer metrics along two criteria: 1) Reliability and 2) Validity. **Reliability** refers to measurement precision/consistency. **Validity** is concerned with what is being measured. Providing evidence of reliability and validity of your customer metrics is essential towards establishing a solid set of customer metrics for your CEM program. See Chapters 26 and 27 for a fuller discussion of reliability and validity, respectively.

Exploring the reliability and validity of your current customer metrics has a couple of extra benefits. First, these types of analyses can improve the measurement properties of your current customer metrics by identifying unnecessary questions. Second, reliability and validity analysis can improve the overall customer survey by identifying CX questions that do not help explain customer loyalty differences. Removal of specific CX questions can significantly reduce survey length without loss of information.

4. How useful is the customer metric?

While customer metrics can be **used** for many types of analyses (e.g., driver, segmentation), their **usefulness** is demonstrated by the number and types of insights they provide. Your validation efforts to understand the quality of the customer metrics create a practical framework for making real organizational changes. Specifically, by understanding the causes and consequences of the customer metric, you can identify/create customer-centric operational metrics to help manage call center performance, understand how changes in the customer metric correspond to changes in revenue and identify customer-focused training needs and standards for employees.

Examples

Below are two articles on the development and validation of four metrics. One article focuses on three related customer metrics. The other article focuses on an employee metric (Yes, the same criteria apply to employee metrics.).

In each article, I present the necessary information needed to critically evaluate each metric: 1) Clear definition of the metrics, 2) description of how metrics are calculated, 3) measurement properties (reliability/ validity), 4) show that metrics are related to important outcomes (e.g., revenue, employee satisfaction). The articles are:

- **Hayes, B.E. (2011). Lessons in loyalty. Quality Progress, March, 24-31.** Paper discusses the development and validation of the RAPID Loyalty approach. Three reliable customer loyalty metrics are predictive of different types of business growth.

- **Hayes, B. E. (1994). How to measure empowerment. Quality Progress, 27(2), 41-46.** Paper discusses need to define and measure empowerment. Researcher develops reliable measure of employee perceptions of empowerment, the Employee Empowerment Questionnaire (EEQ). The EEQ was related to important employee attitudes (job satisfaction).

Summary

A customer metric is good when: 1) it is supported with a **clear definition** of what it measures and what is does not measure; 2) there is a clear method of **how the metric is calculated**, including all items and how they are combined; 3) there is good **reliability and validity evidence** regarding how well the customer metric measures what it is supposed to measure; 4) it is **useful** in helping drive real internal changes (e.g., improved marketing, sales, service) that lead to measurable business growth (e.g., increased revenue, decreased churn).

Using customer metrics that meet these criteria will ensure your CEM program is effective in improving how you manage the customer relationship. Clear definitions of the metrics and accompanying descriptions of how they are calculated help improve communications regarding customer feedback. Different employees, across job levels or roles, can now speak a common language about feedback results. Establishing the reliability and validity of the metrics gives senior executives the confidence they need to use customer feedback as part of their decision-making process.

The bottom line is that a good customer metric provides information that is reliable, valid and useful.

Chapter 14: Clarifying Customer Loyalty

"There is only one valid definition of business purpose: to create a customer."

Peter F. Drucker

There seems to be a consensus among customer feedback professionals that business growth depends on improving customer loyalty. It appears, however, that there is little agreement in how they define and measure customer loyalty. In this chapter and next, I examine the concept of customer loyalty, presenting different definitions of this construct. I attempt to summarize their similarities and differences and present a definition of customer loyalty that is based on theory and practical measurement considerations.

The Different Faces of Customer Loyalty

There are many different definitions of customer loyalty. I did a search on Google using "customer loyalty definition" and found the following:

- **Esteban Kolsky** proposes two models of loyalty: emotional and intellectual. In this approach, Kolsky posits that emotional loyalty is about how the customer feels about doing business with you and your products, "loves" what you do and could not even think of doing business with anybody else. Intellectual loyalty, on the other hand, is more transactionally-based where customers must justify doing business with you rather than someone else.

- **Don Peppers** talks about customer loyalty from two perspectives: attitudinal and behavioral. From Peppers' perspective, attitudinal loyalty is no more than customer preference; behavioral loyalty, however, is concerned about actual behaviors regardless of the customers' attitude or preference behind that behavior.

- **Bruce Temkin** proposed that customer loyalty equates to willingness to consider, trust and forgive.

- **Customer Loyalty Institute** states that customer loyalty is "all about attracting the right customer, getting them to buy, buy often, buy in higher quantities and bring you even more customers."

- **Beyond Philosophy** states that customer loyalty is "the result of consistently positive emotional experience, physical attribute-based satisfaction and perceived value of an experience, which includes the product or services." From this definition, it is unclear to me if they view customer loyalty as some "thing" or rather a process.

- **Jim Novo** defines customer loyalty in behavioral terms. Specifically, he states that customer loyalty, "describes the tendency of a customer to choose one business or product over another for a particular need."

These definitions illustrate the ambiguity of the term, "customer loyalty." Some people take an emotional/attitudinal approach to defining customer loyalty while others emphasize the behavioral aspect of customer loyalty. Still others define customer loyalty in process terms.

Emotional Loyalty

Customers can experience positive feelings about your company/brand. Kolsky uses the word, "love," to describe this feeling of emotional loyalty. I think that Kolksy's two models of customer loyalty (emotional and intellectual) are not really different types of loyalty. They simply reflect two ends of the same continuum. The feeling of "love" for the brand is one end of this continuum and the feeling of "indifference" is on the other end of this continuum.

Temkin's model of customer loyalty is clearly emotional; he measures customer loyalty using questions about willingness to consider, trust and forgive, each representing positive feelings when someone "loves" a company.

Behavioral Loyalty

Customers can engage in positive behaviors toward the company/brand. Peppers believes what is important to companies is customer behavior, what customers do. That is, what matters to business is whether or not customers exhibit positive behaviors toward the company. Also, Novo's definition is behavioral in nature as he emphasizes the word, "choose." While loyalty behaviors can take different forms, they each benefit the company and brand in different ways.

Customer Loyalty as an Attribute about the Customers

To me (due perhaps to my training as a psychologist), customer loyalty is best conceptualized as an attribute about the customer. Customer loyalty is a quality, characteristic or thing about the customer that can be measured. Customers can either possess high levels of loyalty or they can possess low levels of loyalty, whether it is an attitude or behavior. While the process of managing customer relationships is important in understanding how to increase customer loyalty (Customer Loyalty Institute, Beyond Philosophy), it is different from customer loyalty.

Definition of Customer Loyalty

Considering the different conceptualizations of customer loyalty, I offer a definition of customer loyalty that incorporates prior definitions:

> Customer loyalty is the degree to which customers experience positive feelings for and exhibit positive behaviors toward a company/brand.

This definition reflects an attribute or characteristic about the customer that supports both attitudinal and behavioral components of loyalty. This definition of customer loyalty is left generally vague to reflect the different positive emotions (e.g., love, willingness to forgive, trust) and behaviors (e.g., buy, buy more often, stay) that customers can experience.

In the next chapter, I will present a customer loyalty measurement framework that will help clarify this definition. This framework will shed light on the meaning of customer loyalty and how businesses can benefit by taking a more rigorous approach to measuring customer loyalty.

Chapter 15: Customer Loyalty Measurement Framework

"If a measurement matters at all, it is because it must have some conceivable effect on decisions and behavior. If we can't identify a decision that could be affected by a proposed measurement and how it could change those decisions, then the measurement simply has no value."

Douglas W. Hubbard

In the last chapter, I reviewed several definitions of customer loyalty that are being used in business today. It appears that definitions fall into two broad categories of loyalty: **emotional** and **behavioral**. Emotional loyalty is about how customers generally **feel** about a company/ brand (e.g., when somebody loves, trusts, willing to forgive the company/brand). Behavioral loyalty, on the other hand, is about the **actions** customers engage in when dealing with the brand (e.g., when somebody recommends, continues to buy, buys different products from the company/brand). Generally speaking, then, we might think of customer loyalty in the following way:

Customer loyalty is the degree to which customers experience positive feelings for and engage in positive behaviors toward a company/brand.

In this chapter, I will propose a customer loyalty measurement framework to help you understand how to conceptualize and measure customer loyalty. After all, to be of practical value to business, customer loyalty needs to be operationalized (e.g., bringing the concept of loyalty into the measurable world). Once created, these metrics can be used by businesses in a variety of ways to improve marketing, sales, human resources, service and support processes, to name a few. First, I will present two approaches to measuring customer loyalty.

Measurement Approaches

There are two general approaches to measuring customer loyalty: 1) objective approach and 2) subjective (self-reported) approach.

- **Objective measurement approach** includes system-captured metrics that involve hard numbers regarding customer behaviors that are beneficial to the company. Data can be obtained from historical records and other objective sources, including purchase records (captured in a CRM system) and other online behavior. Examples of objective loyalty data include computer generated records of "time spent on the Web site," "number of products/services purchased" and "whether a customer renewed their service contract."

- **Subjective measurement approach** involves "soft" numbers regarding customer loyalty. Subjective loyalty metrics include customers' self-reports of their feelings about the company and behavior toward the company. Examples of subjective loyalty data include customers' ratings on standardized survey questions like, "How likely are you to recommend <Company> to your friends/colleagues?", "How likely are you to continue using <Company>?" and "Overall, how satisfied are you with <Company>?"

While I present two distinct customer loyalty measurement approaches, there are likely gradients of the subjective measurement approach. On one end of the subjective continuum, ratings are more perceptually based (what is typically used today) and, on the other end of the subjective continuum, ratings are more behaviorally based that more closely approximate the objective measurement approach. The objective/subjective dichotomy, however, provides a good framework for discussing measurement approaches.

Before continuing on the measurement of customer loyalty, it is useful to first put customer loyalty in context of how it impacts your business. Generally speaking, companies who have higher levels of customer loyalty also experience faster business growth (See Figure 15.1). Understanding how customer loyalty impacts business growth will help you determine the types of loyalty metrics you need.

Figure 15.1. Companies with higher levels of customer loyalty experience accelerated business growth.

Three Ways to Grow a Business: Retention, Advocacy, Purchasing

Let us take a look at two business models that incorporate customer loyalty as a key element of business growth and company value (See Figure 15.2). The top graph is from Fred Reichheld and illustrates the components that drive company profit. Of the components that contribute to company profits, three of them reflect customer loyalty: retention (measured in years), advocacy (measured as referrals) and expanding purchasing (measured through increased purchases).

Similarly to Reichheld's model, Gupta's Customer Lifetime Value model focuses on customer loyalty as a mediator between what a company does (e.g., business programs) and the company value (see graph on the bottom of Figure 15.2). Again, customer loyalty plays a central role in understanding how to increase firm value. Improving 1) retention behaviors, 2) advocacy behaviors and 3) purchasing behaviors will increase company value.

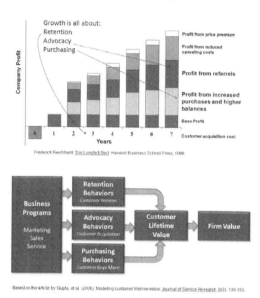

Figure 15.2. Business models illustrate that there are three ways to grow your business. Top Model is from Reichheld, 1996; Bottom model is from Gupta, et al. 2006.

Customer Loyalty Measurement Framework: Operationalizing Customer Loyalty

Our loyalty metrics need to reflect those attitudes and behaviors that will have a positive impact on company profit/value. Knowing that customer loyalty impacts profits/value in three different ways, we can now begin to operationalize our customer loyalty measurement strategy. Whether we use an objective measurement approach or a subjective measurement approach, our customer loyalty metrics need to reflect retention loyalty, advocacy loyalty and purchasing loyalty. Here are a few objective customer loyalty metrics businesses can use:

- Churn rates

- Service contract renewal rates

- Number/Percent of new customers

- Usage metrics - frequency of use/visits, page views

- Sales records - number of products purchased

Here are a few subjective customer loyalty metrics businesses can use:

- likelihood to renew service

- likelihood to leave

- overall satisfaction

- likelihood to recommend

- likelihood to buy different/additional products

- likelihood to expand usage

Customer Loyalty Measurement Framework

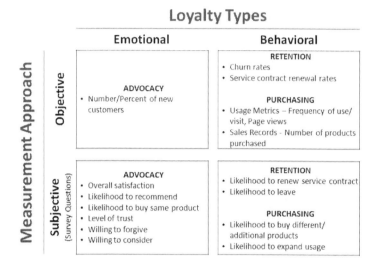

Figure 15.3. Customer Loyalty Measurement Framework: You can measure emotional (e.g., advocacy) and behavioral loyalty (e.g., retention and purchasing) using different measurement approaches (e.g., subjective and objective).

Figure 15.3 illustrates how these loyalty metrics fit into the larger customer loyalty measurement framework of loyalty types and measurement approaches. Each of the customer loyalty metrics above falls into one of the four quadrants.

It is important to point out that the subjective measurement approach is not synonymous with emotional loyalty. Survey questions can be used to measure both emotional loyalty (e.g., overall satisfaction) as well as behavioral loyalty (e.g., likelihood to leave, likelihood to buy different products). In my prior research on measuring customer loyalty, I found that you can reliably and validly measure the different types of loyalty using survey questions.

Looking at the lower left quadrant of Figure 15.3, you see that there are different ways to measure advocacy loyalty. While you might question why "likelihood to recommend" and "likelihood to buy same product" are measuring advocacy loyalty, research shows that they are more closely associated with emotional rather than behavioral loyalty. Specifically, these questions are highly related to "overall satisfaction." Also, factor analysis of several loyalty questions show that these three subjective metrics (sat, recommend, buy) loaded on the same factor. This pattern of results suggests that these questions really are simply measures of the customers' emotional attachment to the company/brand.

I have include the metrics of "level of trust," "willingness to consider" and "willingness to forgive" as emotional loyalty metrics due to their strong emotional nature. Based on what I know about how customers rate survey questions. I suspect these questions would essentially provide the same information as the other questions in the quadrant. That, however, is an empirical question that needs to be tested.

Subjective vs. Objective Measurement Approach

While companies have both objective and subjective measurement approaches at their disposal, surveys remain a popular approach to measuring customer loyalty. In fact, surveys remain the cornerstone of most customer experience management programs.

Companies use customer surveys to measure customer loyalty rather than solely relying on objective metrics of customer loyalty because: 1) Customer surveys allow companies to quickly and easily gauge levels of customer loyalty, 2) Customer surveys can provide rich information about the customer experience that can be used to more easily change organizational business process and 3) Customer surveys provide a forward look into customer loyalty.

RAPID Loyalty Approach

I have conducted research on the subjective approach to measuring customer loyalty over the past few years. Based on the results of this research, I developed a measurement approach that supports the three ways businesses can grow their business: **R**etention, **A**dvocacy and **P**urchasing loyalty. The **RAP**ID loyalty approach includes three metrics, each assessing one of three components of customer loyalty:

- **Retention Loyalty Index (RLI)**: Degree to which customers will remain as customers or not leave to competitors; contains loyalty questions like: renew service contract, leave to competitor (reverse coded – so higher scores always mean higher retention loyalty).

- **Advocacy Loyalty Index (ALI)**: Degree to which customers feel positively toward/will advocate your product/service/brand; contains loyalty questions like: overall satisfaction, recommend, buy again.

- **Purchasing Loyalty Index (PLI)**: Degree to which customers will increase their purchasing behavior; contains loyalty questions like: buy additional products, expand use of product throughout company.

Each of the **RAP**ID loyalty indices has excellent measurement properties; that is, each index is a reliable, valid and useful indicator of customer loyalty and is predictive of future business growth. Specifically, in a nationwide study asking over 1000 customers (See Figure 15.4) about their current network operator, each loyalty index was predictive of different business growth metrics across several US network operators (Alltel, AT&T, Sprint/Nextel, T-Mobile, and Verizon):

- RLI was the best predictor of **future churn rate**

- ALI was a good predictor of **new customer growth**

- PLI was the best predictor of **Average Revenue per User (ARPU) growth**

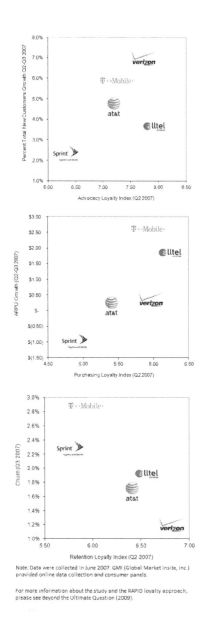

Figure 15.4. The RAPID Loyalty indices (ALI, PLI and RLI), each predict different types of business growth.

The bottom line is that there are three general ways to grow your business: keep customers coming back (**retention**), recommending you to their friends/family (**advocacy**) and expanding their relationship with you by buying different products/services (**purchasing**). To increase company profits/firm value, it is imperative that you measure and optimize each type of customer loyalty. Falling short on one type of customer loyalty will have a deleterious effect on company profit/firm value.

State of Customer Loyalty Measurement

In an informal online poll taken during a talk I gave as part of CustomerThink's Customer Experience Summit 2011, I asked participants about their CEM program's loyalty metrics. While a little over 75% of the respondents said their company uses advocacy loyalty measures, only a third of the respondents indicated that their company uses purchasing loyalty measures (33%) and retention loyalty measures (30%).

Benefits of Measuring Different Types of Customer Loyalty

It appears that most companies' customer loyalty measurement approach is insufficient. Companies who measure and understand different types of customer loyalty and how they are impacted by the customer experience have several advantages over companies who narrowly measure customer loyalty:

- **Target solutions to optimize different types of customer loyalty**. For example, including retention loyalty questions (e.g., "likelihood to quit") and a purchasing loyalty questions (e.g., "likelihood to buy different") can help companies understand why customers are leaving and identify ways to increase customers' purchasing behavior, respectively.

- **Identify key performance indicators (KPIs) for each type of customer loyalty**. Identification of different KPIs (key drivers of customer loyalty) helps companies ensure they are monitoring all important customer experience areas. Identifying and monitoring all KPIs helps ensure the entire company is focused on matters that are important to the customer and his/her loyalty.

- **Obtain more accurate estimates of the Return on Investment (ROI) of improvement initiatives**. Because ROI is the ratio of additional revenue (from increased loyalty) to cost (of initiative), the ROI of a specific improvement opportunity will depend on how the company measures customer loyalty. If only advocacy loyalty is measured, the estimate of ROI is based on revenue from new customer growth. When companies measure advocacy, purchasing and retention loyalty, the estimate of ROI is based on revenue from new *and* existing customer growth.

The primary goal of CEM is to improve customer loyalty. Companies that define and measure customer loyalty narrowly are missing out on opportunities to fully understand the impact that their CEM program has on the company's bottom line. Companies need to ensure they are comprehensively measuring all facets of customer loyalty. A poor customer loyalty measurement approach can lead to sub-optimal business decisions, missed opportunities for business growth and an incomplete picture of the health of the customer relationship.

Summary

Customer loyalty is a very fuzzy concept. With various definitions of customer loyalty floating around in the literature, it is difficult to know what one is talking about when one uses the term, "customer loyalty." I tried to clarify the meaning of customer loyalty by consolidating different customer loyalty definitions into two general customer loyalty types: emotional loyalty and behavioral loyalty.

Additionally, I discussed two measurement

approaches that companies can utilize to assess customer loyalty: objective measurement approach and subjective measurement approach.

Finally, I offered a customer loyalty measurement framework to help companies think about customer loyalty more broadly and help them identify customer loyalty metrics to help them better measure and manage different types of business growth: acquiring new customers (Advocacy), retaining existing customers (Retention) and expanding the relationship of existing customers (Purchasing).

Chapter 16: Measuring Customer Loyalty

"Measurement is the first step that leads to control and eventually to improvement. If you can't measure something, you can't understand it. If you can't understand it, you can't control it. If you can't control it, you can't improve it."

H. James Harrington

Customer loyalty is the leading indicator of business growth. In fact, a main reason why companies implement CEM programs is to improve customer loyalty. Based on a 2010 study by Gleanster, asking 276 companies about their CEM initiative, a majority of the loyalty leading companies said they implemented their program to increase customer loyalty, increase customer retention and increase customer satisfaction.

There are many different ways customers can engage in loyalty behaviors toward your company or brand. They can remain a customer for a long time. They can recommend you to their colleagues and friends. They can even show their loyalty by purchasing additional products/services from you. These loyalty behaviors, in turn, drive different types of business growth: overall customer growth, new customer growth, and average revenue per customer.

Customer relationship surveys, the foundation of many CEM programs, are used to measure customer loyalty, along with other important customer variables (e.g., satisfaction with their experience). Including the right loyalty questions in your customer survey is essential to an effective CEM program. Companies use these surveys to understand and diagnose problem areas that, when fixed, will increase customer loyalty.

Not all Loyalty Questions are Created Equal

I developed a set of customer loyalty questions that measure different types of customer loyalty: retention, advocacy and purchasing.

Retention Loyalty: the extent to which customers remain customers and/or do not use a competitor

- **How likely are you to switch to another provider?** (0 - Not at all likely to 10 - Extremely likely)

- **How likely are you to renew your service contract?** (0 - Not at all likely to 10 - Extremely likely)

Advocacy Loyalty: the extent to which customers advocate your product and/or brand

- **How likely are you to recommend us to your friends/colleagues?** (0 - Not at all likely to 10 - Extremely likely)

- **Overall, how satisfied are you with our performance?** (0 - Extremely dissatisfied to 10 - Extremely satisfied)

Purchasing Loyalty: the extent to which customers increase their purchasing behavior

- **How likely are you to purchase different solutions from us in the future?** (0 - Not at all likely to 10 - Extremely likely)

- **How likely are you to expand the use of our products throughout company?** (0 - Not at all likely to 10 - Extremely likely)

While I prefer to use an 11-point scale for my surveys, other scales can also be used (5-point, 7-point). For the interested reader, I refer you to the book, Measuring Customer Satisfaction and Loyalty, for a deeper discussion on the topic of different measurement scales.

Using Different Types of Loyalty Questions

Selecting the right customer loyalty questions for your survey requires careful thought about your customers and your business. Think about how your customers are able to show their loyalty toward your company and include loyalty questions that reflect those loyalty behaviors you want to manage and change. Additionally, consider your business growth strategy and current business environment. Think about current business challenges and select loyalty questions that will help you address those challenges. For example, if you have a high churn rate, you might consider using a retention loyalty question to more effectively identify solutions to increase customer retention. Additionally, if you are interested in increasing ARPU (average revenue per customer), you might consider including a purchasing loyalty question.

How does Product and Service Experience Impact Each Type of Customer Loyalty?

Two years ago, Mob4Hire, a global crowd-sourced testing and market research community, and I conducted a worldwide survey, asking respondents' about their experience with and loyalty towards their current wireless service provider. To measure the product and service experiences, respondents were asked to indicate their agreement about statements that describes their provider (1 to 5 - higher scores indicate agreement and better customer experience). As a measure of the **product experience**, we averaged respondent's ratings across two questions: 1) good coverage in my area and 2) reliable service (few dropped calls). As a measure of the **service experience**, we averaged respondent's ratings about their provider's representatives across 5 areas: 1) responds to needs, 2) has knowledge to answer questions, 3) was courteous, 4) understands my needs and 5) always there when I need them. The survey also asked about the respondents' loyalty toward their wireless service provider across the three types of loyalty: 1) retention, 2) advocacy and 3) purchasing.

To index the degree of impact that each customer experience dimension has on customer loyalty, I simply correlated the ratings of each customer experience dimension (Coverage/Reliability; Customer Service) with each of the three loyalty measures (Retention, Advocacy, Purchasing). I did this analysis for the entire dataset and then for each of the wireless service providers who had more than 100 respondents. Figure 16.1 contains the results for the impact of Coverage/ Reliability on customer loyalty.

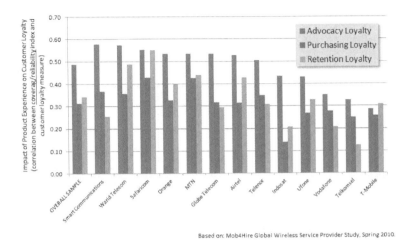

Based on: Mob4Hire Global Wireless Service Provider Study, Spring 2010.

Figure 16.1. Impact of Product Experience on Retention, Advocacy and Purchasing Loyalty.

As you can see in Figure 16.1, using the entire sample (far left bars), the product experience has the largest impact on advocacy loyalty ($r = .49$), followed by retention ($r = .34$) and purchasing ($r = .31$) loyalty. Similarly, in Figure 16.2, using the entire sample (far left bars), the service experience has the largest impact on advocacy loyalty ($r = .48$), followed by purchasing ($r = .34$) and retention loyalty ($r = .32$). Generally speaking, while improving the product and service experience will have the greatest impact on advocacy loyalty, improvement in these areas will have an impact, albeit a smaller one, on purchasing and retention loyalty. I find this pattern of results in other industries as well.

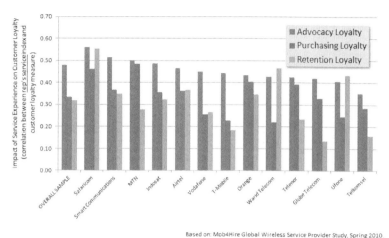

Based on: Mob4Hire Global Wireless Service Provider Study, Spring 2010

Figure 16.2. Impact of Service Experience on Retention, Advocacy and Purchasing Loyalty. Click image to enlarge.

Looking at individual wireless service providers in Figure 16.1 and Figure 16.2, however, we see exceptions to this rule (Providers were ordered by their Advocacy Loyalty scores.). For example, we see that improving the product experience will have a comparable impact on different types of loyalty for specific companies (Figure 1 - T-Mobile, Safaricom). Additionally, we see that improving the service experience will have a comparable impact on different types of loyalty for specific companies (Figure 16.2 - Safaricom, MTN, Orange, Warid Telecom, Telenor, and Ufone).

The value of improving the service experience is different across companies depending on the types of customer loyalty it impacts. For example, improving the service experience is much more valuable for Safaricom than it is for T-Mobile. Improving the service experience will greatly impact all three types of customer loyalty for Safaricom and only one for T-Mobile. I suspect the reasons for variability across providers in what drives their customer loyalty could be due to company maturity, the experience delivery process, market pressures and customer type. Deeper analyses (e.g., stepwise regression, path analysis) of these data for specific providers could help shed light on the reasons.

Why do we use surveys to measure customer loyalty?

Companies track objective measures of customer loyalty to help them monitor the health of the customer relationship. Some objective customer loyalty metrics are:

- Customer retention/defection rates

- New customer growth

- Average revenue per user (ARPU)

Despite the existence of these (and other) objective metrics of customer loyalty, customer relationship surveys remain a frequently used way to assess customer loyalty. Measures of customer loyalty typically take the form of questions that ask the customer to indicate his or her likelihood of engaging in specific types of behaviors, those deemed important to the company/brand. For each objective loyalty metric above, we have a corresponding customer loyalty question:

- How likely are you to switch providers in the next 12 months?

- How likely are you to recommend <Company> to your friends/colleagues?

- How likely are you to buy different/additional products from <Company>?

Here are three reasons why companies use customer surveys to measure customer loyalty rather than solely relying on objective metrics of customer loyalty:

- **Customer surveys allow companies to quickly and easily gauge levels of customer loyalty**. Companies may not have easy access to objective customer loyalty data or may simply not even gather such data.

- **Results from customer surveys can be more easily used to change organizational business process.** Customer surveys commonly include questions about customer loyalty as well as the customer experience (e.g., product, service, support). Used jointly, these questions can be used (e.g., driver analysis, segmentation analysis) to identify reasons why customers are loyal or disloyal.

- **Customer surveys provide a forward look into customer loyalty.** Because objective loyalty metrics are tracked after the loyalty behavior has occurred (typically at the end of each quarter), objective customer loyalty metrics provide a backwards look into customer loyalty levels (e.g., defection rates, repurchase rates). Customer surveys, however, allow companies to examine customer loyalty in real-time. Surveys solicit questions regarding expected levels of loyalty-related behavior and provide opportunities for companies to "look into the future" regarding customer loyalty.

Summary

Companies that narrowly define customer loyalty are missing out on opportunities to fully understand the impact that their CEM program has on the company's bottom line. You need to ensure that you are comprehensively measuring all facets of customer loyalty. A poor customer loyalty measurement approach can lead to sub-optimal business decisions, missed opportunities for business growth and an incomplete picture of the health of the customer relationship.

Chapter 17: Measuring Customer Loyalty in Non-Competitive Environments

"The world is so competitive, aggressive, consumed, selfish and during the time we spend here we must be all but that."

José Mourinho

In some types of companies/industries where competition is non-existent, the aforementioned customer loyalty triad (e.g., retention, advocacy, purchasing) needs to be reevaluated, modified and expanded. Consider **regulated** industries (e.g., utilities, trash collection), **regulatory** agencies (e.g., licensing boards) and **government** agencies (e.g., Internal Revenue Service and Medicare), where customers *do not have a choice*; customers / members have to use these entities, for example, to acquire basic services, practice a specialty (e.g., medicine/law) and receive healthcare benefits, respectively.

How can customer loyalty apply to these types of entities when their customers may not have other options? In an excellent and insightful article (Beyond Mere Customer Retention (2008) in Quirks, Parcenka conceptualized customer loyalty in the energy/utilities industry, a regulated industry, as consisting of three types of customer loyalty:

- **Expansion**: Degree to which a customer is likely to increase the level of business he or she is doing with a company

- **Compliance or influence**: Degree to which a customer is likely to comply with company requests or be influenced by the company in a way that benefits the company

- **Advocacy**: Degree to which a customer is willing to speak favorably about a company to friends, colleagues or others

Taking this comprehensive approach to conceptualizing customer loyalty in non-competitive environments, companies can measure a variety of customer behaviors that benefit the company/agency/ entity. Based on the work by Parcenka, I crafted some loyalty questions that these companies can use to measure customer loyalty (using a 0 - Not at all likely to 10 - Extremely likely scale).

Loyalty Questions for Regulated Industries

- How likely are you to sign up for different programs we offer? (Expansion)

- How likely are you to use us as a consultant when you are selecting products/services from a third party? (Expansion)

- How likely are you to comply with the agency's advice in regulatory matters in your field? (Compliance/Influence for utilities)

- How likely are you to seek our advice/expertise on matters in your field? (Compliance/Influence)

- How likely are you to provide testimonials about us? (Advocacy)

Loyalty Questions for Regulatory Industries

- How likely are you to sign up for different programs we offer? (Expansion)

- How likely are you to use us as a consultant when you are selecting products/services from a third party? (Expansion)

- How likely are you to comply with the agency's advice in regulatory matters in your field? (Compliance/Influence)

- How likely are you to seek the agency's advice/expertise on matters in your field? (Compliance/Influence)

- How likely are you to support the agency's position or action on licensing-related public issues? (Advocacy)

- How likely are you to provide testimonials about positive experiences with the agency? (Advocacy)

- How likely are you to support the agency's issues on changing licensing processes (e.g., new tests)? (Advocacy)

Loyalty Questions for Government Agencies

- How likely are you to sign up for different programs the agency offers? (Expansion)

- How likely are you to seek the agencies advice/expertise on healthcare matters? (Compliance/Influence in Medicare)

- How likely are you to follow the agency's advice about your healthcare? (Compliance/Influence in Medicare)

- How likely are you to support the agency's position or action on issues related to your benefits? (Advocacy in Medicare)

- How likely are you to provide testimonials about positive experiences with us? (Advocacy in Medicare)

While these loyalty questions are not meant to be comprehensive, they do provide a good starting point for companies/agencies/entities to think about different positive behaviors (e.g., loyalty behaviors) they want their customers to exhibit. When generating loyalty questions for your specific needs, Parcenka says to consider the following things:

- What does the agency want from customers? Customers have many different ways they can support an agency. Consider broadening your idea about customer loyalty and think about how different types of customer behaviors could benefit your company.

- How can customers support the agency's mission?

- What can customers do to help agency better serve them?

- What can customers do to help agency minimize cost of doing business?

- How do your ideal customers behave differently than your less-than-ideal customers? The behaviors that distinguish these groups would be candidates for helping you to generate customer loyalty questions.

Summary

In a competitive environment, customer loyalty behaviors come in a variety of different forms (recommendations, satisfaction, continued patronage, increase purchases, share of wallet). Each type of loyalty is responsible for different types of business growth. In a non-competitive environment, you can still measure different types of customer loyalty behaviors.

Think about how your customers show their loyalty and include corresponding questions that ask about their likelihood of engaging in those loyalty behaviors. Including a "likelihood to seek agency's advice" question and a "likelihood to sign up for different program" question can help you understand why customer are seeking your advice and identify ways to increase customers' usage of your agency, respectively. In non-competitive environments, companies can still find value in measuring and understanding different types of customer loyalty behaviors beyond recommending behaviors or other commonly tracked loyalty behaviors.

Chapter 18: Measuring the Customer Experience

"The most serious mistakes are not being made as a result of wrong answers. The truly dangerous thing is asking the wrong questions."

Peter Drucker

A formal definition of customer experience, taken from Wikipedia, states that customer experience is: "The sum of all experiences a customer has with a supplier of goods or services, over the duration of their relationship with that supplier." In practical terms, customer experience is the customer's perception of, and attitude about, different areas of your company or brand across the entire customer lifecycle (e.g., marketing, sales and service).

We know that the customer experience has a large impact on customer loyalty. Customers who are satisfied with the customer experience buy more, recommend you and are easier to up/cross-sell than customers who are dissatisfied with the customer experience. Your goal for the customer relationship survey, then, is to ensure it includes customer experience questions asking about important customer touch points.

Customer Experience Questions

Customer questions typically account for most of the questions in customer relationship surveys. There are two types of customer experience questions: General and Specific. **General questions ask customers to rate broad customer touch points. Specific customer experience questions focus on specific aspects of the broader touch points.** As you see in Table 18.1, general customer experience questions might ask the customers to rate their satisfaction with 1. Product Quality, 2. Account Management, 3. Technical Support and so on. Specific customer experience questions ask customers to rate their satisfaction with detailed aspects of each broader customer experience area.

Area	General CX Questions	Specific CX Questions
Product	1. Product Quality	1. Reliability of product 2. Features of product 3. Ease of using the product 4. Availability of product
Account Management	2. Sales / Account Management	1. Knowledge of your industry 2. Ability to coordinate resources 3. Understanding of your business issues 4. Responds quickly to my needs
Technical Support	3. Technical Support	1. Timeliness of solution provided 2. Knowledge and skills of personnel 3. Effectiveness of solution provided 4. Online tools and services

Table 18.1. General and Specific Customer Experience Questions. In practice, survey asks customers to rate their satisfaction with each area.

I typically see both types of questions in customer relationship surveys for B2B companies. The general experience questions are presented first and then are followed-up with specific experience questions. As such, I have seen customer relationship surveys that have as little as five (5) customer experience questions and other surveys that have 50+ customer experience questions.

General Customer Experience Questions

Here are some general customer experience questions I typically use as a starting point for helping companies build their customer survey. As you can see in Figure 18.1, these general questions address broad areas across the customer lifecycle, from marketing and sales to service.

While specific customer experience questions are designed to provide greater understanding of customer loyalty, it is important to consider their usefulness. Given that we already have general customer loyalty question in our survey, do we need the specific questions? **Do the specific questions help us explain customer loyalty differences above what we know through the general questions?**

General Customer Experience Questions

Overall, how satisfied are you with each area?

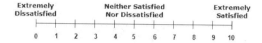

1. Ease of doing business
2. Sales / Account Management
3. Product Quality
4. Service Quality
5. Technical Support
6. Communications from the Company
7. Future Product/Company Direction

Figure 18.1. General Customer Experience Questions

Customer Experience Questions Predicting Customer Loyalty

To answer these questions, I analyzed four different B2B customer relationship surveys, each from four different companies. These companies represented midsize to large enterprise companies. Their semi-annual customer surveys included a variety of loyalty questions and specific and general customer experience questions. The four companies had different combinations of general (5 to 7) and specific customer experience questions (0 to 34).

The goal of the analysis was to **show whether the inclusion of specific experience questions added to our understanding of customer loyalty differences beyond what the general experience questions explained.** The results of the analysis are presented in Figure 18.2. Through stepwise regression analysis, I first calculated the percent of variance in customer loyalty that is explained by the general customer experience questions (green area). Then, I calculated the percent of variance in customer loyalty explained by the specific questions above what the general questions explained (blue area). Clearly, the few general experience questions explain a lot of the variability in customer loyalty (42% to 85%) while the specific customer experience questions account for very little extra (2% to 4%).

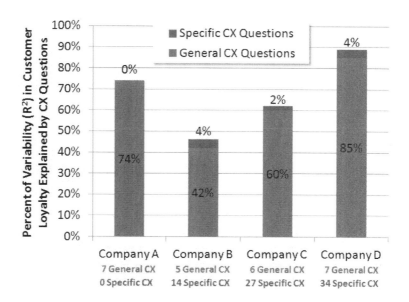

Figure 18.2. Impact of General and Specific Customer Experience Questions on Customer Loyalty (overall sat, recommend, buy again). Percent of variability is based on stepwise regression analysis.

Efficient Customer Relationship Surveys

We may be asking customers too many questions in our relationship surveys. Short relationship surveys, using general experience questions, provide great insight into understanding how to improve customer loyalty. Asking customers about specific, detailed aspects about their experience provides very little additional information about what drives customer loyalty.

Customers' memories are fallible. Given the non-trivial time between customer relationship surveys (up to a year between surveys), customers are unable to make fine distinctions regarding their experience with you (as measured in your survey). This scenario might be a good example of the halo effect, the idea that a global evaluation of a company/brand (e.g., great product) influences opinions about their specific attributes (e.g., reliable product, ease of use).

Customers' ratings about general customer experience areas explain as much of the differences in customer loyalty as we are able to with customer experience questions. Short relationship surveys allow customers the optimal way to give their feedback on a regular basis. Not only do these short relationship surveys provide deep customer insight about the causes of customer loyalty, they also enjoy higher response rates and show that you are considerate of customers' time.

Chapter 19: Measuring Your Relative Performance

"The competitor to be feared is one who never bothers about you at all, but goes on making his own business better all the time."

Henry Ford

Companies continually look for ways to increase customer loyalty (e.g., recommendations, retention, continue buying, purchase different/additional offerings). Companies typically measure the satisfaction with the customer experiences (e.g., product, service, support) and use that information to target improvement efforts in areas that will maximize customer loyalty. Keiningham et al. (2011) argue that focusing on your absolute improvements in customer experience is not enough to drive business growth. What is necessary to increase business growth is to improve your performance relative to your competitors. He and his colleagues found, in fact, that a company's ranking (against the competition) was strongly related to share of wallet of their customers. In their two-year longitudinal study, they found that top-ranked companies received greater share of wallet of their customers compared to bottom-ranked companies.

A way to improve customer loyalty, then, is to increase your standing relative to your competition. To improve your ranking, you need to understand two pieces of information: 1) how your customers rank you relative to competitors they have used and 2) the reasons behind your ranking.

Relative Performance Assessment (RPA): A Competitive Benchmarking Approach

The Relative Performance Assessment (RPA) was designed to help companies understand their relative ranking against their competition and identify ways to increase their ranking. In its basic form, the RPA method requires two additional questions in your customer relationship survey:

- **RPA Question 1: What best describes our performance compared to the competitors you use?** This question allows you to gauge each customer's perception of where they think you stand relative to other companies/brands in their portfolio of competitors they use. The key to RPA is the rating scale. The rating scale allows customers to tell you where your company ranks against all others in your space. The 5-point scale for the RPA is:

1. <your company name> is the worst

2. <your company name> is worse than most

3. <your company name> is average (about the same as others)

4. <your company name> is better than most

5. <your company name> is the best

- **RPA Question 2: Please tell us why you think that "insert answer to question above".** This question allows each customer to indicate the reasons behind his/her ranking of your performance. The content of the customers' comments can be aggregated to identify underlying themes to help diagnose the reasons for high rankings (e.g., ranked the best / better than most) or low rankings (ranked the worst / worse than most).

In addition to these two questions, companies can also ask their customers about the current (and past) use of specific competitors:

- **Please tell us what other competitors**

you currently use or have used. This question allows you to identify how your customer's ranking of your performance is influenced by specific competitors. The response options for this question could be a simple checklist of your competitors.

Utility of the Relative Performance Assessment (RPA)

The value of any business solution is reflected in the insight it provides you. Here is how the RPA can help you.

- **Improve marketing communications**: Understand why customers gave you the top ranking (rated you "the best"). These customers' comments define your competitive advantage (at least to your customers). Identify themes across these customers and use them to guide the content in your marketing communications to prospects.

- Identify how to improve **your competitive ranking**: Understand why customers rank you near the bottom of the pack. These customers' comments define your competitors' strength (compared to you) and can help you identify business areas where you need to make improvements in order to improve your ranking against competing brands.

- **Estimate your industry percentile ranking**: Your relative performance is indexed as a percentile rank. This percentile rank, expressed as a percentage, indicates where you stand in the distribution of all other competitors. The percentile rank can vary from 0% to 100%, and a higher percentile rank indicates better relative performance. A percentile rank of 80%, for example, indicates you are better than 80% of the rest. A percentile rank of 20% indicates you are better than 20% of the rest. The ratings can be translated into percentile values using the following values: the worst = 0; worse than most = 25; average = 50; better than most = 75; the best = 100. The average value across your respondents on this question represents your industry percentile rank. I call this index the Customers' Perception of Percentile Rank (C-PeRk) score.

- **C-PeRk Score as a Key Business Metric**: Typical relationship surveys allow customers to rate their satisfaction with your **absolute** performance. By supplementing these key customer-centric metrics with the C-PeRk score, companies can now measure and track insights regarding their **relative** performance compared to the competition.

RPA in Practice

Here is an example of the RPA method that was used in a relationship survey for a B2B software company. This particular company had customers that used several competitors, so the RPA method was appropriate. The results in Figure 19.1 show that, on average, customers think the company is a typical supplier in the space, with a few customers indicating extreme ratings.

Additionally, similar to the findings in the Keiningham study, I found that the RPA was related to loyalty measures (see Figure 19.2). That is, customers who rank a company high also report high levels of customer loyalty toward that company. Conversely, customers who rank a company low also report low levels of customer loyalty toward that company. This relationship is especially strong for Advocacy and Purchasing loyalty.

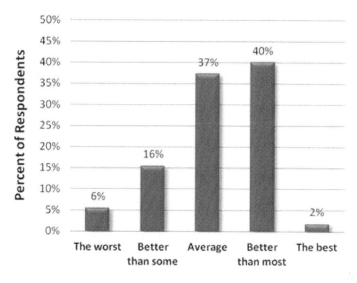

Figure 19.1. Percent of responses regarding relative performance

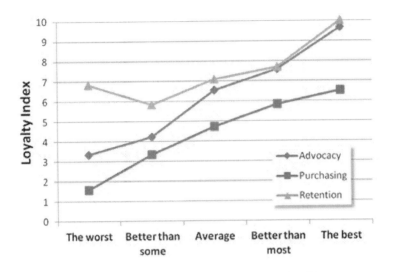

Figure 19.2. Relative performance (RPA) is related to different types of customer loyalty.

Relative Performance, Customer Experience and Customer Loyalty

To understand the importance of the relative performance, I wanted to determine how well the RPA explained customer loyalty after accounting for the effects of the customer experience. Along with the RPA, this relationship survey also included seven (7) general customer experience questions (e.g., product quality, support quality, communications from the company) that allowed the customer to rate their experience across different customer touch points and 5 customer loyalty questions measuring the three types of customer loyalty: retention, advocacy and purchasing.

Understanding the causes of customer loyalty is essential to any Customer Experience Management (CEM) program. To be of value, the RPA needs to explain differences in customer loyalty beyond traditional customer experience measures. I ran a stepwise regression analysis for each loyalty question to see if the Relative Performance Assessment helped us explain customer loyalty differences beyond what can be explained by general experience questions.

For each customer loyalty question, I plotted the percent of variance in loyalty that is explained by the general questions and the one RPA question. As you can see in Figure 19.3, the 7 general experience questions explain advocacy loyalty better than they do for purchasing and retention loyalty. Next, looking at the RPA question, we see that it has a significant impact on purchasing loyalty behaviors. In fact, the RPA improves the prediction of purchasing loyalty by almost 50%. This finding shows us that 1) there is value in asking your customers about your relative performance and 2) improving the company's ranking will increase purchasing loyalty and share of wallet.

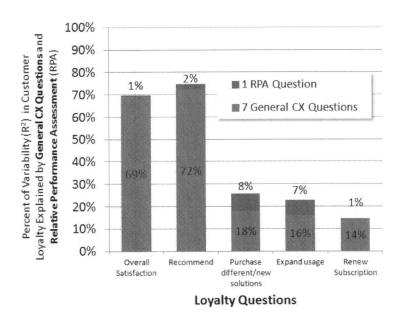

Figure 19.3. Relative performance (RPA) helps explain purchasing loyalty behavior. Improving relative performance will increase purchasing loyalty and share of wallet.

Understanding your Ranking

Further analysis of the data can help you understand your competitive (dis)advantage and the reasons behind your ranking. First, correlate the experience ratings with the RPA to see which customer experience area has the biggest impact on your relative performance. Second, content analysis of the second RPA question (e.g., why customers gave that ranking) can reveal the reasons behind your ranking. Applying both of these methods on the current data, I found a common product-related theme that might be responsible for their ranking. Specifically, results showed that the biggest customer experience driver of relative performance was product quality. For this company, improving product quality will improve the company's relative standing compared to the competition.

Summary

The relative performance of your company (compared to competitors) is related to customer loyalty. Companies that have higher industry rankings receive more share of wallet from their customers than companies who have lower industry rankings. Traditional customer experience metrics simply track your companies' performance. Augment this information by asking customers about your performance relative to competitors.

Chapter 20: Your Optimal Customer Relationship Survey

"We listened to what our customers wanted and acted on what they said. Good things happen when you pay attention."

John F. Smith

Even though the customer relationship survey is only one component of a CEM program, it oftentimes provides the main data collection source of many businesses' customer experience management (CEM) programs. Consequently, creating an effective customer relationship survey is critical to the program's success. Based on the prior chapters on different types of metrics, I put it all together here to show what an optimal survey looks like.

A customer relationship survey is essentially a series of questions that your customers answer about their experience with you. When creating/editing the content of your customer relationship survey, you need to consider both analytic (e.g., empirical/psychometric) and practical (e.g., survey length) issues to maximize the value you receive from the survey. By applying analytics to survey questions, I will illustrate why short surveys provide just as much information as longer surveys.

The Optimal Customer Relationship Survey

The optimal customer relationship survey can be divided into four (4) sections, each with its specific questions. These survey sections are:

- Customer Loyalty

- Customer Experience

- Competitive Benchmark

- Additional Questions (e.g., open-ended, demographics, targeted)

1. Customer Loyalty

Customer loyalty behaviors come in a variety of different forms (recommendations, satisfaction, continued patronage, increase purchases, share of wallet). Each type of loyalty is responsible for different types of business growth.

Think about how your customers show their loyalty and include corresponding questions that ask about their likelihood of engaging in those loyalty behaviors.

Including specific loyalty questions will help you better pinpoint a solution to optimize different types of customer loyalty. Including a "likelihood to quit" question and a "likelihood to buy different" question can help you understand why customer are leaving and identify ways to increase customers' purchasing behavior, respectively.

As a starting point, consider including a loyalty question for each of the three general types of loyalty behaviors: retention, advocacy and purchasing. Sample loyalty questions for each type of loyalty are:

- How likely are you to switch providers? (retention)

- How likely are you to renew your service contract? (retention)

- How likely are you to recommend us to your friends? (advocacy)

- Overall, how satisfied are you with <Company Name>? (advocacy)

- How likely are you to purchase different solutions from <Company Name>? (purchasing)

- How likely are you to expand use of <Company Name's> products throughout company? (purchasing)

Ratings scales are from 0 (Not at all likely) to

10 (Extremely likely) for the likelihood questions, 0 (Extremely Dissatisfied) to 10 (Extremely Satisfied) for the satisfaction question.

2. Customer Experience

This area of the survey is the meat of most customer relationship surveys. The customer experience is the customer's perception of, and attitude about, specific areas (customer experience dimensions) of your company/brand. Customer experience questions ask the customers to rate various customer touch points.

As I illustrated in Chapter 18, only a handful of customer experience questions (around 5 to 7 items) capture the majority of information you need to understand drivers of customer loyalty. While some industries might have their own unique general customer experience questions, there are general customer experience questions that apply to most industries. Here are a few examples:

- Ease of doing business

- Sales / Account Management

- Product Quality

- Service Quality

- Technical Support

- Communications from the Company

- Future Product/Company Direction

For each question, the customer is asked, "How satisfied are you with each of the following areas regarding your experience with <Company>?" Customers are provided a rating scale that ranges from 0 (Extremely Dissatisfied) to 10 (Extremely Satisfied).

3. Competitive Benchmark

Competitive benchmarking is a useful way to help you understand where you fit in the mix of competitors and help you improve your marketing, sales and service efforts. Let survey respondents compare your company to a comparison group (e.g., your competitors or industry leader). The comparative response options and specific scale values allow your customers to provide valuable benchmark information about your company and your competitors. Sample competitive benchmark questions are:

- How do our products compare with the alternatives?

- What best describes our performance compared to the competitors you use?

- How does <Company Name's> services compare to other suppliers?

4. Additional Questions

Companies may have a need to ask additional questions. These questions, driven by specific business needs, can include demographic questions, open-ended questions, and targeted questions.

Some companies do not need to ask any demographic questions as these data are housed in the CRM system and are automatically linked up to customers' survey responses. When you do not have easy access to this type of information, ask a few key questions about your customers. These questions will help you segment your customers to help you understand different constituencies. Typical questions in B2B relationship surveys include:

- Time as a customer

- Job function (e.g., Marketing, Sales, IT, Service)

- Job level (executive, director, manager, individual contributor)

- Level of influence in purchasing decisions of <Company Name> solutions (Primary decision maker, Decision influencer, No influence)

Include one or two open-ended questions that allow respondents to provide additional feedback in their own words. Depending on how the questions are phrased, customers' remarks can provide additional insight about the health of the customer relationship. Text analytics help you understand both the primary content of words as well as the sentiment behind them. To understand potential improvement areas, a question I commonly use is:

- If you were in charge of <Company Name>, what improvements, if any, would you make?

Customer relationship surveys can be used to collect feedback about specific topics that are of interest to executive management. Give careful consideration about asking additional questions. As with any survey question, you must know exactly how the data from the questions will be used to improve customer loyalty. Some popular topics of interest include 1) measuring perceived benefits of solutions, 2) measuring perceived value and 3) measuring customer engagement (that'll be a future post). Some sample questions are:

- How much improvement did you experience in productivity due to <Company Name's> solutions?

- How satisfied are you with the price of the solution given the value received?

Summary

Customer relationship surveys deliver business intelligence that help companies improve the customer experience and increase customer loyalty. An effective survey will include questions that measure 1) different types of customer loyalty, 2) general measures of the customer experience and 3) competitive benchmarks.

Chapter 21: Summarizing your Metric: Mean or Net Score?

"Statistics are used much like a drunk uses a lamppost: for support, not illumination."

Vin Scully

Customer metrics are numerical scores or indices that summarize customer feedback results for a given customer group or segment. Customer metrics are typically calculated using customer ratings of survey questions. One of the criteria for a good customer metric is how the customer metric calculated. There needs to be a clear, logical method of how the metric is calculated, including all items (if there are multiple items) and how they are combined.

Calculating Likelihood to Recommend Customer Metric

Let's say that we conducted a survey asking customers the following question: **"How likely are you to**

recommend COMPANY ABC to your friends/ colleagues?" Using a rating scale from 0 (not at all likely) to 10 (extremely likely), customers are asked to provide their rating. How should you calculate a metric to summarize the responses? What approach gives you the most information about the responses?

There are different ways to summarize these responses to arrive at a customer metric. Four common ways to calculate a metric are:

1. **Mean Score**: This is the arithmetic average of the set of responses. The mean is calculated by summing all responses and dividing by the number of responses. Possible scores can range from 0 to 10.

2. **Top Box Score**: The top box score represents the percentage of respondents who gave the best responses (either a 9 or 10 on a 0-10 scale). Possible percentage scores can range from 0 to 100.

3. **Bottom Box Score**: The bottom box score represents the percentage of respondents who gave the worst responses (0 through 6 on a 0-10 scale). Possible percentage scores can range from 0 to 100.

4. **Net Score**: The net score represents the difference between the Top Box Score and the

Bottom Box Score. Net scores can range from -100 to 100. While the net score was made popular by the Net Promoter Score camp, others have used a net score to calculate a metric. While the details might be different, net scores take the same general approach in their calculations (percent of good responses - percent of bad responses). For the remainder, I will focus on the Net Promoter Score methodology.

Comparing the Customer Metrics

To study these four different ways to summarize the "Likelihood to recommend" question, I wanted to examine how these metrics varied over different companies/ brands. Toward that end, I combined a few large studies that included a variety of companies. Each study was an independent examination about consumer attitudes toward either their PC Manufacturer or Wireless Service Provider. Here are the specifics for each study:

- **PC manufacturer:** Survey of 1058 general US consumers in Aug 2007 about their PC manufacturer. All respondents for this study were interviewed to ensure they met the correct profiling criteria, and were rewarded with an incentive for filling out the survey. Respondents were ages 18 and older. GMI (Global Market

Insite, Inc., www.gmi-mr.com) provided the respondent panels and the online data collection methodology.

- **Wireless service provider:** Survey of 994 US general consumers in June 2007 about their wireless provider. All respondents were from a panel of General Consumers in the United States ages 18 and older. The potential respondents were selected from a general panel which is recruited in a double opt-in process; all respondents were interviewed to ensure they meet correct profiling criteria. Respondents were given an incentive on a per-survey basis. GMI provided the respondent panels and the online data collection methodology.

- **Wireless service providers:** Survey of 5686 worldwide consumers from spring 2010 about their wireless provider. All respondents for this study were rewarded with an incentive for filling out the survey. Respondents were ages 18 or older. Mob4Hire provided the respondent panels and the online data collection methodology.

From these three studies across nearly 8000

respondents, I was able to calculate the four customer metrics for 48 different brands/companies. Companies that had 30 or more responses were used for the analyses. Of the 48 different brands, most were from the Wireless Service provider industry (N = 41). The remaining seven were from the PC industry. Each of these 48 brands had four different metrics calculated on the "Recommend" question. The descriptive statistics of the four metrics and the correlations across the 48 brands appear in Table 21.1.

| | Mean | N | SD | Correlations | | | |
				1	2	3	4
1 Recommend - Mean Score	6.98	48	0.71	1.00			
2 Recommend - Net Score (NPS)	-3.66	48	22.86	0.97	1.00		
3 Recommend - Top 2 Box (% 9 and 10)	36.67	48	12.41	0.91	0.97	1.00	
4 Recommend - Bottom 7 Box (% 0 thru 6)	36.32	48	11.33	-0.96	-0.96	-0.85	1.00

Table 21.1. Correlations among different summary metrics of the same question (likelihood to recommend).

As you can see in Table 21.1, the four different customer metrics are highly related to each other. The correlations among the metrics vary from .85 to .97 (the negative correlations with Bottom 7 Box indicate that the bottom box score is a measure of badness; higher scores indicate more negative customer responses).

These extremely high correlations indicate that these four metrics tell us roughly the same thing about the 48 brands. That is, brands with high Mean Scores are those that are getting high Net Scores, high Top Box Scores and Low Bottom Box scores. These are overly redundant metrics.

When you plot the relationship between the Mean Scores and Net Scores, you can clearly see the close relationship between the two metrics (see Figure 21.1.). In fact, the relationship between the Mean Score and NPS is so high, that you can, with great accuracy, predict your NPS score (y) from your Mean Score (x) using the regression equation in Figure 21.1.

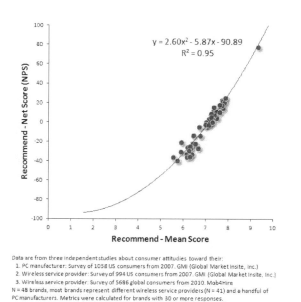

$$y = 2.60x^2 - 5.87x - 90.89$$
$$R^2 = 0.95$$

Data are from three independent studies about consumer attitudies toward their:
1. PC manufacturer: Survey of 1058 US consumers from 2007. GMI (Global Market Insite, Inc.)
2. Wireless service provider: Survey of 994 US consumers from 2007. GMI (Global Market Insite, Inc.)
3. Wireless service provider: Survey of 5686 global consumers from 2010. Mob4Hire
N = 48 brands, most brands represent different wireless service providers (N = 41) and a handful of PC manufacturers. Metrics were calculated for brands with 30 or more responses.

Figure 21.1. Scatter plot of two ways to summarize the "Likelihood to Recommend" question (Mean Score and Net Score (NPS))

Mean Score v Net Promoter Score v Top/Bottom Box

The "Likelihood to Recommend" question is a commonly used question in customer surveys. But what is the most efficient way to summarize the results? Based on the analyses, here are some conclusions regarding the different methods.

1. Net Scores do not provide any additional insight beyond what we know by Mean Scores

Recall that the correlation between the Mean Score and the NPS across the 48 brands was **.97!** Both metrics are telling you the same thing about how the brands are ranked relative to each other. The mean score uses all the data to calculate the metric while the NPS ignores specific customer segments. So, what is the value of the NPS?

2. Net Scores are ambiguous/difficult to interpret

An NPS value of 15 could be derived from a different combination of promoters and detractors. For example, one company could arrive at an NPS of 15 with 40% promoters and 25% detractors while another company could arrive at the same NPS score of 15 with 20% promoters and 5% detractors. Are these two companies with the same NPS really the same?

Also, more importantly, the ambiguity of the NPS lies in the lack of a scale of measurement. While the calculation of the NPS is fairly straightforward (e.g., take the difference of two values to arrive at a score), the score itself becomes meaningless because the difference transformation creates an entirely new measurement scale that ranges from -100% to 100%. So, what does a score of zero (0) indicate? Is that a bad score? Does that mean a **majority of your customers would not recommend you**?

A mean score, on the other hand is very easy to interpret. The mean is on the same scale of measurement as the rating scale itself (0 to 10) and the reader intuitively understands the meaning. So, when we report a mean of 7.1, the reader understands that the majority of scores probably lie around the rating of 7.

Understanding what an NPS of zero (0) indicates can only occur when you map the NPS value back to the original scale of measurement (0 to 10 likelihood scale). A scatter plot (and corresponding regression equation) of NPS and Mean Score is presented in Figure 21.2.

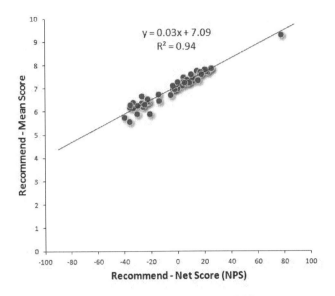

Data are from three independent studies about consumer attitudes toward their:
1. PC manufacturer: Survey of 1058 US consumers from 2007. GMI (Global Market Insite, Inc.)
2. Wireless service provider: Survey of 994 US consumers from 2007. GMI (Global Market Insite, Inc.)
3. Wireless service provider: Survey of 5686 global consumers from 2010. Mob4Hire
N = 48 brands, most brands represent different wireless service providers (N = 41) and a handful of
PC manufacturers. Metrics were calculated for brands with 30 or more responses.

Figure 21.2. Scatter plot of two ways to summarize the "Likelihood to Recommend" question (Net Score (NPS) and Mean Score) for the Recommend Question

If we plug zero (0) into the equation, your expected Mean Score would be 7.1, indicating that a majority of your customers would recommend you (mean score is above the midpoint of the rating scale). If you know your NPS score, you can estimate your mean score using this formula. Even though it is based on a narrowly defined sample, I think the regression model is more a function of the constraints of the calculations than a characteristic of the sample. I think it will provide some good approximation. If you try it, let me know how accurate it is.

3. Top/Bottom Box provides information about clearly defined customer segments

Segmenting customers based on their survey responses makes good measurement and business sense. Using top box and bottom box methods helps you create customer segments (e.g., disloyal, loyal, very loyal) that have meaningful differences across segments in driving business growth. So, rather than creating a net score from the customer segments (see number 2), you are better off simply reporting the absolute percentages of the customer segments.

Summary

Communicating survey results requires the use of metrics. Summary metrics are used to track progress and benchmark against loyalty leaders. There are a variety of ways to calculate summary metrics (e.g., mean score, top box, bottom box, net score), yet the results of my analyses show that these metrics are telling you the same thing.

There are clear limitations to the NPS metric. The NPS does not provide any additional insight about customer loyalty beyond what the mean score tells us. The NPS is ambiguous and difficult to interpret. Without a clear unit of measurement for the difference score, the meaning of an NPS score (say, 24) is unclear. The components of the NPS, however, are useful to know.

I typically report survey results using mean scores and top/middle/bottom box results. I find that combining these methods help paint a comprehensive picture of customer loyalty. Figure 21.3 includes a graph that summarizes the results of responses across three different types of customer loyalty. I avoid using net scores.

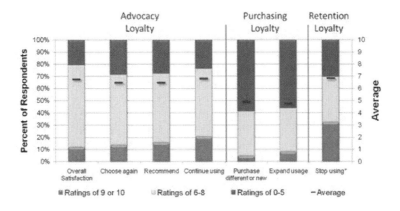

Figure 21.3. Reporting loyalty results using mean scores and top/middle/bottom box scores (customer segments).

Chapter 22: The Problems with the Net Promoter Score

"Facts do not cease to exist because they are ignored."

Aldous Huxley

In 2003, the Net Promoter **Score** (NPS) was formally introduced by Fred Reichheld. His and his co-developer's claim that the NPS was the best predictor of business growth (e.g., better than overall satisfaction) was never replicated. I have presented this information elsewhere, but, since I am continually asked about my views of the NPS, the content is warranted here to help remind you of the NPS past. I am guessing the Net Promoter Score developers have not forgotten the past. Why else do you think they changed the meaning of NPS to Net Promoter **System**?

The Net Promoter Score (NPS) is used by many of today's top businesses to monitor and manage customer relationships. Fred Reichheld and his co-developers of the NPS say that a single survey question, "How likely are you to recommend Company Name to a friend or colleague?", on which the NPS is based, is the only loyalty metric companies need to grow their company. Despite its widespread adoption by major brands, the NPS is now at the center of a debate regarding its merits.

NPS Methodology

The NPS is calculated from a single loyalty question, "How likely are you to recommend us to your friends/ colleagues?" Based on their rating of this question using a 0 to 10 likelihood scale where 0 means "Not at all Likely" and 10 means "Extremely Likely," customers are segmented into three groups: 1) Detractors (ratings of 0-6), 2) Passives (ratings of 7-8) and 3) Promoters (ratings of 9-10). A company can calculate its Net Promoter Score by simply subtracting the proportion of Detractors from the proportion of Promoters.

$$NPS = prop(Promoters) - prop(Detractors)$$

NPS Claims

Fred Reichheld, the co-developer of the NPS (along with Satmetrix and Bain & Company) has made very strong claims about the advantage of the NPS over other loyalty metrics. Specifically, they have said:

- The NPS is "the best predictor of growth,"

(Reichheld, 2003)

- The NPS is "the single most reliable indicator of a company's ability to grow" (Netpromoter.com, 2007)

- "Satisfaction lacks a consistently demonstrable connection to... growth" (Reichheld, 2003)

Reichheld support these claims with research displaying the relationship of NPS to revenue growth. In compelling graphs, Reichheld (2006) illustrates that companies with higher Net Promoter Scores show better revenue growth compared to companies with lower Net Promoter Scores. Reichheld sites only one study conducted by Bain & Associates (co-developers of the NPS) showing the relationship between satisfaction and growth to be 0.00.

Scientific Challenges to NPS Claims

Researchers, pointing out the NPS claims are only supported by Reichheld and his co-developers, have conducted rigorous scientific research on the NPS with startling results. For example, Keiningham et al. (2007), using the same technique employed by Reichheld to show the relationship between NPS and growth, used survey results from the American Customer Satisfaction Index (ACSI) to create scatterplots to show the relationship between satisfaction and growth. Looking at the personal computer industry, they found that **satisfaction is just as good as the NPS at predicting growth**. Keiningham et al. (2007) found the same pattern of results in other industries (e.g., insurance, airline, ISP). In all cases, satisfaction and NPS were comparable in predicting growth.

Still, other researchers (Morgan & Rego, 2006) have shown that other conventional loyalty measures (e.g., overall satisfaction, likelihood to repurchase) are comparable to NPS in predicting business performance measures like market share and cash flow.

Contrary to Reichhheld, other researchers, in fact, have found that customer satisfaction is consistently correlated with growth (Anderson, et al., 2004; Fornell, et al., 2006; Gruca & Rego, 2005).

Problems with NPS Research

The recent scientific, peer-reviewed studies cast a shadow on the claims put forth by Reichheld and his cohorts. In fact, there is no published empirical finding supporting the superiority of the NPS over other conventional loyalty metrics.

Keiningham et al. (2007) aptly point out that there may be research bias by the NPS developers. There seems to be a lack of full disclosure from the Net Promoter camp with regard to their research. The Net Promoter developers, like any research scientists, need to present their analysis to back up their claims and refute the current scientific research that brings their methodological rigor into question. To date, they have not done so. Instead, the Net Promoter camp only points to the simplicity of this single metric which allows companies to become more customer-centric. That is not a scientific rebuttal. That is marketing.

Chapter 23: Simplifying Loyalty Driver Analysis

"There is nothing so terrible as activity without insight."

Johann Wolfgang von Goethe

In their attempts to improve systemic problems, companies use customer feedback data to **identify where customer experience improvement efforts will have the greatest return on investment (ROI)**. Facing a tidal wave of customer feedback data, how do companies make sense of the data deluge? One way is to use Loyalty Driver Analysis, a strategic business intelligence solution that distills the feedback data into meaningful information. This method provides most of the insight you need to direct your customer experience improvement efforts to business areas (e.g., product, service, account management, marketing) that matter most to your customers.

The Survey Data

Your customer experience management program collects

customer feedback using a customer relationship survey that measures satisfaction with the customer experience and customer loyalty. Specifically, these measures are:

- **Satisfaction with the customer experience for each of seven (7) business areas**: Measures that assess the quality of the customer experience. I focus on these seven customer experience areas: 1) Ease of Doing Business, 2) Account Management, 3) Overall Product Quality, 4) Customer Service, 5) Technical Support, 6) Communications from the Company and 7) Future Product/Company Direction. Using a 0 (Extremely Dissatisfied) to 10 (Extremely Satisfied) scale, higher ratings indicate a better customer experience (higher satisfaction).

- **Customer Loyalty**: Measures that assess the likelihood of engaging in different types of loyalty behaviors. I use three measures of customer loyalty: 1) Advocacy Loyalty, 2) Purchasing Loyalty and 3) Retention Loyalty. Using a 0 (Not at all likely) to 10 (Extremely likely) scale, higher ratings indicate higher levels of customer loyalty.

Summarizing the Data

You need to understand only two things about each of the seven business areas: 1) How well you are performing in each area and 2) How important each area is in predicting customer loyalty:

- **Performance:** The level of performance is summarized by a summary statistic. Different approaches provide basically the same results; pick one that senior executives are familiar with and use it. Some use the mean score (sum of all responses divided by the number of respondents). Others use the "top-box" approach which is simply the percent of respondents who gave you a rating of, say, 9 or 10 (on the 0-10 scale). So, you will calculate seven (7) performance scores, one for each business area. Low scores reflect a poor customer experience while high scores reflect good customer experience.

- **Impact**: The impact on customer loyalty can be calculated by simply correlating the ratings of the business area with the customer loyalty ratings. This correlation is referred to as the "derived importance" of a particular business area. So, if the survey has measures of seven (7) business areas, we will calculate seven (7) correlations. The correlation between the satisfaction scores of a business area and the loyalty index indicates the degree to which performance on the business area has an impact on customer loyalty behavior. Correlations can be calculated using Excel or any statistical software package. Higher correlations (max is 1.0) indicate a strong relationship between the business area and customer loyalty (e.g., business area is important to customers). Low correlations (near 0.0) indicate a weak relationship between the business area and customer loyalty (e.g., business area is not important to customers).

Graphing the Results: The Loyalty Driver Matrix

So, we now have the two pieces of information for each business area: 1) Performance and 2) Impact. Using both the performance index and derived importance for a business area, we plot these two pieces of information for each business area.

The abscissa (x-axis) of the Loyalty Driver Matrix is the performance index (e.g., mean score, top box percentage) of the business areas. The ordinate (y-axis) of the Loyalty Driver Matrix is the impact (correlation) of the business area on customer loyalty.

The resulting matrix is referred to as a **Loyalty Driver Matrix** (see Figure 23.1). By plotting all seven data points, we can visually examine all business areas at one time, relative to each other.

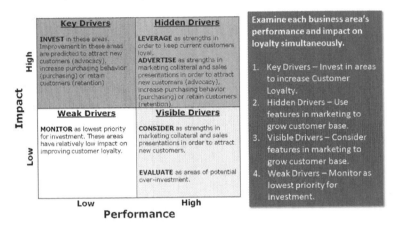

Figure 23.1. Loyalty Driver Matrix is a Business Intelligence Solution

Understanding the Loyalty Driver Matrix: Making Your Business Decisions

The Loyalty Driver Matrix is divided into quadrants using the average score for each of the axes. Each of the business areas will fall into one of the four quadrants. The business decisions you make about improving the customer experience will depend on the quadrant in which each business area falls:

- **Key Drivers**: Business areas that appear in the upper left quadrant are referred to as Key Drivers. Key drivers reflect business areas that have both a **high impact on loyalty** and have **low performance ratings** relative to the other business areas. These business areas reflect good areas for potential customer experience improvement efforts because we have ample room for improvement and we know business areas are linked to customer loyalty; when these business areas are improved, you will likely see improvements in customer loyalty (attract new customers, increase purchasing behavior and retain customers).

- **Hidden Drivers**: Business areas that appear in the upper right quadrant are referred to as Hidden Drivers. Hidden drivers reflect business areas that have a **high impact on loyalty** and have **high performance ratings** relative to other business areas. These business areas reflect the company's strengths that keep the customer base loyal. Consider using these business areas in marketing and sales collateral in order to attract new customers, increase purchasing behaviors or retain customers.

- **Visible Drivers**: Business areas that appear in the lower right quadrant are referred to as Visible Drivers. Visible drivers reflect business areas that have a **low impact on loyalty** and have **high performance ratings** relative to other business areas. These business areas reflect the company's strengths. These areas may not impact loyalty but they are areas in which you are performing well. Consider using these business areas in marketing and sales collateral in order to attract new customers.

- **Weak Drivers**: Business areas that appear in the lower left quadrant are referred to as Weak Drivers. Weak drivers reflect business areas that have a **low impact on loyalty** and have **low performance ratings** relative to other business areas. These business areas are lowest priorities for investment. They are of low priority because, despite the fact that performance is low in these areas, these areas do not have a substantial impact on whether or not customers will be loyalty toward your product/company.

Example

A software company wanted to understand the health of their customer relationship. Using a customer relationship survey, they collected feedback from nearly 400 of their customers. Applying driver analysis to this set of data resulted in the Loyalty Driver Matrix in Figure 23.2. The results of this driver analysis show that **Account Management is a key driver of customer loyalty**; this business area is the top candidate for potential customer experience improvement efforts; it has a large impact on advocacy loyalty AND there is room for improvement.

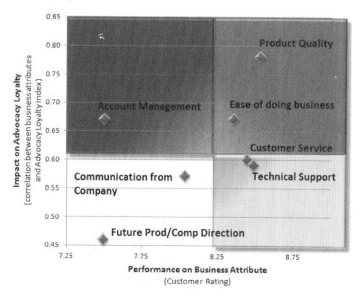

Figure 23.2. Loyalty Driver Matrix for Software Company

While the Loyalty Driver Matrix helps steer you in the right direction with respect to making improvements, you must consider the cost of making improvements. Senior management needs to balance the insights from the feedback results with the cost (labor hours, financial resources) of making improvements happen. Maximizing ROI occurs when you are able to minimize the costs while maximizing customer loyalty. Senior executives of this software company implemented product training for their Account teams. This solution was inexpensive relative to the expected gains they would see in new customer growth (driven by advocacy loyalty). Additionally, the company touted the **ease of doing business** with them as well as the quality of their **products**, **customer service** and **technical support** in their marketing and sales collateral to attract new customers.

Although not presented here, the company also calculated two additional driver matrices based on the results using the other two loyalty indices (purchasing loyalty and retention loyalty). These three Loyalty Driver Matrices provided the foundation for making improvements that would impact different types of customer loyalty.

Summary

Loyalty Driver Analysis is a strategic business intelligence solution that helps companies understand and improve the health of the customer relationship. The matrix is based on two key pieces of information: 1) Performance of the business area and 2) Impact of the business area on customer loyalty. Using these two key pieces of information for each business area measured, senior executives are able to make better strategic business decisions to improve customer loyalty and accelerate business growth.

Chapter 24: Using Word Clouds

"Of all of our inventions for mass communication, pictures still speak the most universally understood language."

Walt Disney

I continually look for ways to present data in ways that are both informational and visually interesting. My hope is that, if scientific rigor does not capture the readers' attention, the way in which the data are presented will.

I stumbled across the use of word clouds in survey research. Word clouds are used to visualize free form text. A word cloud is a collection of words individually weighted by size that reflect the frequency of occurrence of that word within the body of the text. Word clouds are also referred to as tag clouds or "weighted lists" (see wikipedia.org). While the visual appearance or layout of a word cloud can be driven by various properties of the words (list words alphabetically, randomly, by size), other non-word-related properties can be used to enhance the word cloud (font color, intensity, present words horizontally and vertically).

The aforementioned word cloud on which I stumbled last month reflected the summary of a one-question survey that required a one-word answer. The resulting word cloud of answers was essentially an artful frequency distribution of each answer (the larger the font size, the more frequently that word was mentioned by respondents). The combination of form, color, size, and positioning of words worked well to keep my attention.

After a quick search, I found two sites (wordle.net and tagxedo.com) to help me generate word clouds. I have included a few here to illustrate different applications of word clouds in CEM programs.

Example 1: What do you do?

I created a word cloud using the content from my Web site. Figure 24.1 is the result of one of the word clouds that was generated by wordle.net. This picture, I thought, was a creative way to convey what I do. I use this word cloud to quickly convey my professional interests to customers and prospects in a visually stunning way. What will you find if you generate a word cloud on your company's CEM documentation?

Figure 24.1. Business Over Broadway: It's All About The Customer - Based on Web site content. Click image to enlarge.

Example 2: Personal Computer Manufacturers: "Getting to Love"

A few years ago, I conducted a survey of about 1000 US consumers on their experience with their personal computer. In addition to structured customer loyalty and customer experience questions (provided quantitative ratings), the survey included one open-ended question that asked the respondent, "What is the most important area of improvement for your personal computer manufacturer?" The resulting word cloud of the responses is presented in Figure 24.2. I call this word could, "Getting to Love," to convey what PC manufacturers need to do to get customers to love them. I included the brand logos of the major PC manufacturers that were represented in the survey; they are ranked, top-down, based on their loyalty ratings from the survey.

Figure 24.2. Personal Computer Manufacturers: Getting to Love - Based on B.O.B. PC Manufacturer Study of US Consumers, Summer 2007.

Example 3: Wireless Service Providers: "Getting to Love" and "They Can't Build an App for That"

Mob4Hire and I conducted a worldwide survey to assess loyalty toward wireless service providers. A total of 5686 "Mobsters" completed the web-based survey. Similar to the study above, the survey included one open-ended question that asked the respondent, "What is the most important area of improvement for your provider?" Using the responses to this question (and with the help of Photoshop), The "Getting to Love" word cloud for this questions appears in Figure 24.3.

Figure 24.3. Wireless Service Providers: Getting to Love - Based on Mob4Hire Global Wireless Service Provider Study, Spring 2010.

I created another word cloud to satisfy the creative urge in me. Using the same text, I generated a simple word cloud, created an image of a generic smartphone (Thank you, Photoshop!) and put together the image in Figure 24.4. I call this one: "You Can't Build an App for That."

Figure 24.4. Wireless Service Providers: You Can't Build An App for That - Based on Mob4Hire Global Wireless Service Provider Study, Spring 2010.

Drive Interest in the Voice of the Customer

Supporting your statistical analyses with a visually stunning representation of your customers' comments goes a long way in generating interest in your CEM program. Capturing the essence of customer sentiment, customer-based word clouds can be used to facilitate

231

group discussions about the customer and help communicate survey results throughout the company.

I have already incorporated word clouds into reporting customer relationship survey results. While they are not meant to replace a more thorough examination of text content using text analytic methods, customer word clouds are an excellent complement to the more statistically rigorous methods.

Word Clouds for Building a Customer-Centric Culture

I think that the main benefit of using word clouds in CEM programs is one of efficiently communicating a customer-centric culture to all constituencies. I recall how Siebel Systems used customer-related art work for their offices to keep the customers in the minds of all employees (Customer logos, magazine covers highlighting customers and even customer commendation letters about a company employee were all used as artwork throughout Siebel Systems buildings.). Word clouds of customer comments can play a similar role.

Section 5: Applied Research

"Learn from yesterday, live for today, hope for tomorrow. The important thing is to not stop questioning."

Albert Einstein

Research comes in different forms. Review of existing literature is one way to learn about facts. Another form of research is to examine a set of data (in our case, customer feedback data) with our analytic tools to uncover facts. In this section of the book, I will present best practices regarding customer research and how loyalty leading companies approach their data. The prior chapters on linkage analysis might be useful to review as data integration is paramount to establishing a sound research.

I will illustrate how companies can assess the quality of their CEM program; this validation process is useful when the results of your program are challenged, by both internal parties (e.g., constituencies who are impacted by the customer feedback results) and external parties (business analysts who talk about the quality of your company). I will provide an example of how Oracle uses their data to uncover insights about how operational metrics impact customer satisfaction.

Chapter 25: Best Practices in Applied Research

"Research is what I'm doing when I don't know what I'm doing."

Wernher von Braun

Customer-focused research using the customer feedback data can provide additional insight into the needs of the customer base and increases the overall value of the CEM program. This research extends well beyond the information that is gained from the typical reporting tools that summarize customer feedback with basic descriptive statistics.

Loyalty leaders regularly conduct applied research using their customer feedback data. Typical research projects can include creating customer-centric business metrics, building incentive compensation programs around customer metrics, and establishing training criteria that has a measured impact on customer satisfaction. Sophisticated research programs require advanced knowledge of research methods and statistics. Deciphering signal from noise in the data require more than the inter-ocular test (eyeballing the data).

Loyalty leaders link their customer feedback data to other data sources. Once the data are merged (see Chapters 9, 10 and 11 regarding different data models to help examine specific questions), analysis can be conducted to help us understand the causes (operational, constituency) and consequences (financial) of customer satisfaction and loyalty.

Loyalty leaders can use the results of these types of studies to:

- Support business case of CEM program (financial linkage)

- Identify objective, operational metrics that impact customer satisfaction and manage employee performance using these customer-centric metrics (operational linkage)

- Understand how employees and partners impact customer satisfaction to ensure proper employee and partner relationship management (constituency linkage)

A list of best practices in Applied Research appears in Table 25.1.

Best Practices	The specifics...
15. Ensure results from customer feedback collection processes are reliable, valid and useful	Conduct a validation study, verifying the reliability, validity and usefulness of customer feedback metrics. This study is used to support (and dispute any challenges regarding) the use of these customer metrics to manage the company, create summary statistics for use in executive reporting and company dashboards.
16. Identify linkage between customer feedback metrics and operational metrics	Identify operational metrics that are related to customer feedback metrics. Because of their reliability and specificity, these operational customer-centric metrics are good candidates for use in employee incentive programs.
17. Regularly conduct applied customer-focused research	Build a comprehensive research program using the customer-centric metrics (and other business metrics) to get deep insight regarding the business processes.
18. Identify linkage between customer feedback metrics and business metrics	Illustrate that financial metrics (e.g., profit, sales, and revenue) are related to customer feedback metrics. Often times, this type of study can be used as a business case to demonstrate value of the customer feedback program.
19. Identify linkage between customer feedback metrics and other constituency's attitudes	Identify factors of constituency attitudes (e.g., employee and partner satisfaction) that are linked to customer satisfaction/loyalty. Used to properly manage employee and partner relationships to ensure high customer loyalty. Surveying all constituencies in the company ecosystem helps ensure all parties are focused on the customers and their needs.
20. Understand customer segments using customer information	Compare customer groups across key customer metrics to identify key differences across groups (e.g., satisfaction, and loyalty). This process helps identify best practices internally among customer segments.

Table 25.1. Best Practices in Applied Research

Summary

Loyalty leaders are excellent examples of customer-centric companies. Compared to their loyalty lagging counterparts, loyalty leading companies embed customer feedback throughout the entire company, from top to bottom. Loyalty leaders use customer feedback to set the vision and manage their business; they also integrate the feedback into daily business processes and communicate all processes, goals and results of the customer program to the entire company. Finally, they integrate different business data (operational, financial, customer feedback), to reveal deep customer insights through in-depth research.

Chapter 26: Assessing the Reliability of your CEM Program

"That which can be asserted without evidence, can be dismissed without evidence."

Christopher Hitchens

Companies rely on different types of statistical analyses to extract information from their customer experience management data. For example, segmentation analysis (using analysis of variance) is used to understand differences across key customer groups. Driver analysis (using correlational analysis) is conducted to help identify the business areas responsible for customer dis/loyalty. These types of analyses are so commonplace that some Enterprise Feedback Management (EFM) vendors include these sorts of analyses in their automated online reporting tools. While these analyses provide good insight, there is still much more you can learn about your customers as well as your CEM program with a different look at your data. We will take a look at reliability analysis.

Reliability Analysis

To understand reliability analysis, you need to look at your customer feedback data through the eyes of a psychometrician, a professional who practices psychometrics. Psychometrics is the science of educational and psychological measurement and is primarily concerned with the development and validation of measurement instruments like questionnaires. Psychometricians apply scientifically accepted standards when developing/evaluating their questionnaires. One important area of focus for psychometricians relates to reliability.

Reliability

Reliability refers to the consistency/precision of a set of measurements. There are four different types (See Figure 26.1) of reliability: 1) inter-rater reliability, 2) test-retest reliability, 3) parallel-forms reliability and 4) internal consistency reliability. Each type of reliability is focused on a different type of consistency/precision of measurement. Each type of reliability is indexed on a 0 (no reliability) to 1.0 (perfect reliability) scale. The higher the reliability index (closer to 1.0), the greater the consistency/precision in measurement.

While there are different kinds of reliability (see Figure 26.1), one in particular is especially important when the customer metric is made up of multiple items (e.g., most commonly, items are averaged to get one overall metric). Internal consistency reliability is a great summary index that tells you if the items should combined together. Higher internal consistency (above .80 is good; 1.0 is the maximum possible) tells you that the items measure one underlying construct; aggregating the items makes sense. Low internal consistency tells you that the items are likely measuring different things and should not be aggregated together.

Four Types of Reliability

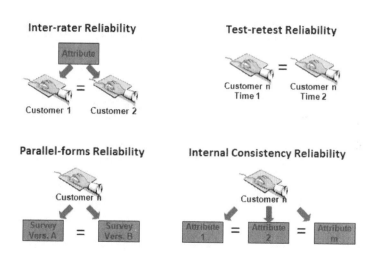

Figure 26.1. Four Types of Reliability

Inter-rater Reliability

Inter-rater reliability reflects the extent to which **Contacts within an Account give similar ratings**. Typically applied in a B2B setting, inter-rater reliability is indexed by a correlation coefficient between different Contacts within each Account across all Accounts (see Figure 26.2 for the data model to conduct this analysis). We do expect the ratings from different Contacts from the same Account to be somewhat similar; they are from the same Account after all.

Data Model for
Inter-rater Reliability Analysis

Type of Contact

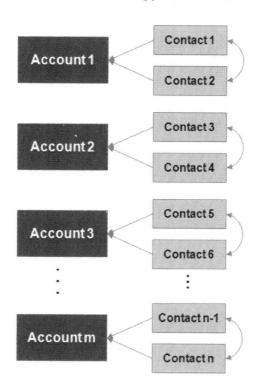

Figure 26.2. Data model for inter-rater reliability analysis

A low inter-rater reliability could reflect a poor implementation of the CEM program across different

Contacts within a given Account. However, a low inter-rater reliability is not necessarily a bad outcome; a low inter-rater reliability could simply indicate: 1) little or no communication between Contacts within a given Account, 2) different Contacts (Business-focus vs. IT-focus) have different expectations regarding your company/brand or 3) different Contacts have different experiences with your company/brand.

Test-retest Reliability

Test-retest reliability reflects the extent to which **customers give similar ratings over a non-trivial time period**. Test-retest reliability is typically indexed by a correlation coefficient between the same raters (customers) across two different time periods (See Figure 26.3 for the data model to conduct this analysis). This reliability index is used as a measure of how stable customers' attitudes are over time. In my experience analyzing customer relationship surveys, I have found that customers' attitudes tend to be somewhat stable over time. That is, customers who are satisfied at Time 1 tend to be satisfied at Time 2; customers who are dissatisfied at Time 1 tend to be dissatisfied at Time 2.

Data Model for
Test-retest Reliability Analysis

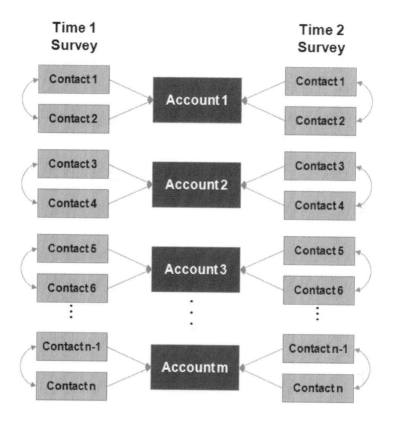

Figure 26.3. Data model for test-retest reliability analysis

High test-retest reliability could be a function of the dispositional tendency of your customers. Research finds that some people are just more negative than others (called negative affectivity). This negative-dispositional tendency impacts all aspects of these people's lives. Some customers are just positive people and will tend to rate things positively (including survey questions); others, who are more negative, will tend to rate things negatively. However, high test-retest reliability could indicate that customers are simply receiving the same customer experience over time. A low test-retest reliability could reflect an inconsistent service delivery process over time.

Parallel-forms Reliability

Parallel-forms reliability reflects the extent to which **customers give similar ratings across two different measures that assess the same thing**. For practical reasons, this form of reliability is not typically examined for CEM programs as companies have only one customer survey they administer to a particular customer. Parallel-forms reliability is typically indexed by a correlation coefficient between the same raters (customers) completing two different measures (given at the same time).

Internal Consistency Reliability

Internal consistency reliability reflects the extent to which customers are consistent in their ratings over different questions. This type of reliability is used when examining a composite score that is made up of several questions. This type of reliability tells us if each question that makes up the composite score measures the same thing. Internal consistency reliability is typically indexed by Cronbach's alpha. The appropriate data model to examine internal consistency is located in Figure 26.4.

Data Model for
Internal Consistency Reliability Analysis

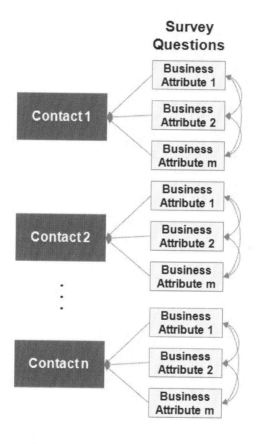

Figure 26.4. Data model for internal consistency reliability analysis.

We expect a relatively high degree of internal consistency reliability for our composite scores (above .80 is a good standard). Low internal consistency reliability indicates that our composite score is likely made up of items that should not be combined together. We always strive to have high internal consistency reliability for our composite customer metrics. Customer metrics with high internal consistency reliability are better at distinguishing people on the continuum of whatever it is you are measuring (e.g., customer loyalty, customer satisfaction). When a relationship between two variables (say, customer experience and customer loyalty) exists in our population of customers, we are more likely to find a statistically significant result using reliable customer metrics compared to unreliable customer metrics.

Summary

Establishing the quality of CEM data requires specialized statistical analysis. Reliability reflects the degree to which your CEM program generates consistent results. Assessing different types of reliability provide different types of insight about the quality of your CEM program. Inter-rater reliability indicates whether different Contacts within Accounts give similar feedback. Test-retest reliability indicates whether customers (Contacts) give similar ratings over time. Internal consistency reliability indicates whether your aggregated score (averaged over different questions) makes statistical sense. Assessing the reliability of the data generated from your CEM program needs to be an essential part of your program to ensure your program delivers reliable information to help senior executives make better, customer-centric business decisions.

Chapter 27:
Assessing the Validity of your CEM Program

"The good thing about science is that it's true whether or not you believe in it."

Neil DeGrasse Tyson

Customer feedback is used to make many different business decisions, including, setting strategy, compensating employees, allocating company resources, changing business processes, benchmarking best practices and developing employee training programs just to name a few. The quality of the customer feedback directly impacts the quality of these business decisions. Poor quality feedback will necessarily lead to sub-optimal business decisions while high quality feedback will lead to optimal business decisions.

As I discussed in the previous chapter, reliability refers to the degree to which your CEM program delivers consistent results. While determining the reliability of your CEM program is essential, you need to evaluate the validity of your CEM program.

Validity

Validity refers to the degree to which customer ratings generated from your CEM program measure what they are intended to measure. Because of the subjective nature of customer feedback ratings, we rely on special types of evidence to determine the extent to which ratings reflect underlying customer attitudes/feelings. We want to answer the question: "Are we really measuring "satisfaction," "customer loyalty," or other important customer variables with our customer feedback tool?

Unlike reliability, there is no single statistic that provides an overall index of the validity of the customer ratings. Rather, the methods for gathering evidence of validity can be grouped into three different approaches: content-related, criterion-related, and construct-related. When determining the validity of the customer ratings, you will likely rely on a variety of these three methods:

1. Content-related Evidence

Content-related evidence is concerned with the degree to which the items in the customer survey are representative of a "defined universe" or "domain of content." The domain of content typically refers to all possible questions that could have been used in the customer survey. The goal of content-related validity is to have a set of items that best represents all the possible questions that could be asked of the customer.

For customer feedback tools, the important content domain is all possible questions that could have been asked of the respondents. Two methods can be used to understand the content-related validity of the customer survey. First, review the process by which the survey questions were generated. The review process would necessarily include documentation of the development of the survey questions. Survey questions could be generated based on subject matter experts (SMEs) and/ or actual customers themselves. Subject matter experts (SMEs) typically provide the judgment regarding the content validity of the feedback tool.

Second, a random sample of open-ended comments from respondents can be reviewed and summarized to determine the general content of these verbatim comments. Compare these general content areas with existing quantitative survey questions to discern the overlap between the two. The degree to which customers' verbatim comments match the content of the quantitative survey questions indicates some level of content validity.

While there are many potential questions to ask your customers, research has shown that only a few general customer experience (CX) questions are needed for a customer survey. These general CX questions represent broad customer touch points (e.g., product, customer support, account management, company communications) across the three phases of the customer lifecycle (marketing, sales and service).

2. Criterion-related Evidence

Criterion-related evidence is concerned with examining the statistical relationship (usually in the form of a correlation coefficient) between customer feedback (typically ratings) and another measure, or criterion. With this type of evidence, what the criterion is and how it is measured are of central importance. The main question to be addressed in criterion-related validity is how well the customer rating can predict the criterion.

The relationship between survey ratings and some external criteria (not measured through the customer survey) is calculated to provide evidence of criterion-related validity. This relationship between survey ratings and some external criterion is typically index using the Pearson correlation coefficient, but other methods for establishing this form of validity can be used. For example, we can compare survey ratings across two *knowingly different groups* that should result in different satisfaction levels (reflected by their survey ratings). Specifically, satisfaction ratings should vary across different "Service Warranty Levels" and "Account Sizes." The different treatment of various customer groups should lead to different customer satisfaction results. In these types of comparisons, Analysis of Variance (ANOVA) can be employed on the data to compare various customer groups. The ANOVA allows you to determine if the observed differences across the customer segments are due to chance factors or are real and meaningful.

3. Construct-related Evidence

Construct-related evidence is concerned with the customer rating as a measurement of an underlying construct and is usually considered the ultimate form of validity. Unlike criterion-related validity, the primary focus is on the customer metric itself rather than on what the scale predicts. Construct-related evidence is derived from both previous validity strategies (e.g., content and criterion). The questions in the survey should be representative of all possible questions that could be asked (content-related validity) and survey ratings should be related to important criteria (criterion-related validity).

Because the goal of construct-related validity is to show that the survey is measuring what it is designed to measure, theoretical models are implicitly used to embed the constructs being measured (e.g., satisfaction, loyalty) into a framework (see Service Delivery Model). In customer satisfaction research, it is widely accepted that customer satisfaction is a precursor to customer loyalty. Consequently, we can calculate the relationship (via Pearson correlation coefficient) between satisfaction ratings and measures of customer loyalty questions (overall satisfaction, likelihood to recommend).

A high degree of correlation between the customer ratings and other scales/measures that purportedly measure the same/similar construct is evidence of construct-related validity (more specifically, convergent validity). Construct-related validity can also be evidenced by a low correlation between the customer ratings (e.g., customer loyalty) and other scales that measure a different construct (e.g., customer engagement) (more specifically, discriminant validity).

Difference between Reliability and Validity

Reliability and validity are both necessary elements to good measurement. Figure 27.1 illustrates the distinction between two criteria for measurement.

Two Measurement Criteria for Customer Metrics

1. Reliability is about precision/consistency of the metric

2. Validity is about meaning of the metric

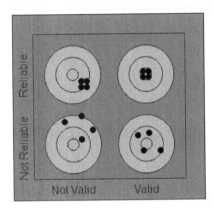

Figure 27.1. Two Measurement Criteria: Reliability is about precision; Validity is about meaning.

The diagram consists of four targets, each with four shots. In the upper left hand target, we see that the there is high reliability in the shots that were fired yet the bull's-eye has not been hit. This is akin to having a scale with high reliability but is not measuring what the scale was designed to measure (not valid). In the lower right target, the pattern indicates that there is little consistency in the shots but that the shots are all around the bull's-eye of the target (valid). The pattern of shots in the lower left target illustrates low consistency/precision (no reliability) and an inability to hit the target (not valid). The upper right pattern of shots at the target represents our goal to have precision/consistency in our shots (reliability) as well as hitting the bull's-eye of the target (validity).

Applications of Reliability and Validity Analysis

The bottom line: a good customer survey provides information that is **reliable**, **valid** and **useful**. Applying psychometric standards like reliability and validity to customer feedback data can help you accomplish and reveal very useful things.

- **Validate the customer feedback process**: When CEM data are used for important business decision (e.g., resource allocation, incentive compensation), you need to demonstrate that the data reflect real customer perceptions about important areas.

- **Improve account management**: Reliability analysis can help you understand the extent of agreement between different Contacts within the same Account. Your account management strategy will likely be different depending on the agreement between Contacts within Accounts. Should each relationship be managed separately? Should you approach the Accounts with a strong business or IT focus?

- **Create/Evaluate customer metrics**: Oftentimes, companies use composite scores (average over several questions) as a key customer metric. Reliability analysis will help you understand which questions can/should be combined together for your customer metric.

- **Modify surveys**: Reliability analysis can help you identify which survey questions can be removed without loss of information; additionally, reliability can help you group questions together that make the survey more meaningful to the respondent.

- **Test popular theories**: Reliability analysis has helped me show that the likelihood to recommend question (NPS) measures the same thing as overall satisfaction and likelihood to buy again. That is why the **NPS is not better** than "overall satisfaction" or "continue to buy" in predicting business growth.

- **Evaluate newly introduced concepts into the field**: One of my biggest pet peeves in the CEM space is the introduction of new metrics/measures **without any critical thinking** behind the metric and what it really measures. For example, I have looked into the measurement of customer engagement via surveys and found that these measures literally have the exact same questions as our traditional measures of customer loyalty (e.g., recommend, buy again, overall satisfaction (please see Gallup's Customer Engagement Overview Brochure for an example). Simply giving a different name to a set of questions does not make it a new variable. In fact, Gallup says nothing about the reliability of their Customer Engagement instrument.

Summary

The ultimate goal of reliability and validity analyses is to provide qualitative and quantitative evidence that the CEM program is delivering precise, consistent and meaningful scores regarding customers' attitudes about their relationship with your company. Establishing the reliability and validating the CEM program needs to be one of the first research projects for any CEM program. A validation study of the CEM program builds confidence that such decisions lead to improved customer loyalty and business success. Validation efforts described here provide an objective assessment of the quality of the program to ensure the data reflect **reliable**, **valid** and **useful** customer feedback.

Chapter 28: How Oracle Uses Big Data to Improve the Customer Experience

"The more data that you have, the better the model that you will be able to build. Sure, the algorithm is important, but whoever has the most data will win."

Gil Elbaz

Customer experience management programs typically rely on customer feedback as their main data source (e.g., social media, customer emails, tech support notes, formal customer surveys). Customer feedback data, however, are only one type of business data that are used to improve business decisions. Fueled by the interest in Big Data (See Chapter 7), companies are now realizing the value of integrating different data with their customer feedback data.

Oracle Understands Value of Integrating Data Silos

Jeb Dasteel, Oracle's Senior Vice President and Chief Customer Officer, understands the value of integrating different data sources with their customer metrics:

> "It is important to understand how the operational measures that we use to drive our business correlate to the satisfaction of our customers. Our studies have helped determine the areas of operational performance that are the key drivers of our customer's satisfaction. This has provided an opportunity to focus our improvement initiatives specifically on those areas that are of greatest importance to our customers."
>
> Jeb Dasteel, SVP, Chief Customer Officer, Oracle from the book, Beyond the Ultimate Question.

By integrating different types of metrics (from disparate data silos), Oracle is able to expand how they think about their customer experience improvement initiatives. Rather than focusing solely on their customer metrics to gain customer insights, Oracle links different data sources to get a holistic understanding of all the business areas that impact customer loyalty. Here is how they accomplished this Big Data project.

Oracle's Service Request Process

Oracle customers can request help in the form of service requests (SRs). The quality of these SRs is typically measured using objective operational metrics that are automatically generated in their CRM system. Oracle's system tracks many operational metrics. For this illustration, we will look at three:

- Total Time to Resolve (Close Date – Open Date)

- Initial Response Time

- Number of SR Ownership Changes

In addition to the operational metrics that are captured as part of their SR process, Oracle solicits feedback from their customers about the quality of their specific SR experience (via transaction-based survey). These customer feedback data are housed in a separate system apart from the operational metrics.

Oracle wanted to understand how their operational metrics were related to satisfaction with the service request.

Data Federation of Operational Metrics and Customer Metrics

Oracle used data federation to pull together metrics from the two disparate data sources (one for operational metrics and one for customer satisfaction metrics). The data were linked together at the transaction level (see Chapter 10, Figure 10.1).

After the data were linked together, segments for each operational variable were created (from low to high values) to understand how customer satisfaction varied over different levels of the operational metric.

Results of Analyses

Analyses revealed some interesting insights about how the three operational metrics impact customer satisfaction with the transaction. The relationship of each operational metric with overall satisfaction with the SR is presented in Figures 28.1, 28.2 and 28.3.

Using Total Time to Resolve the SR, Oracle found that customers were more satisfied with their SRs that were resolved more quickly compared to customers whose SRs took longer to resolve (See Figure 28.1.).

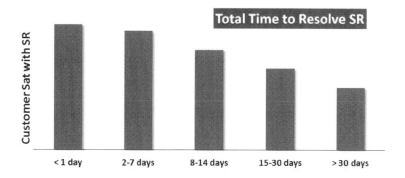

Figure 28.1. Relationship between time to resolve SR and customer satisfaction with SR

Using Initial Response Time to the SR, Oracle found that customers were no more satisfied or dissatisfied with their SRs whether the initial response time was fast or slow (see Figure 28.2.). Despite the expectations that the Initial Response Time to the SR would greatly impact the customers' satisfaction with the SR, this study showed that the initial response time had no impact on the satisfaction of customers.

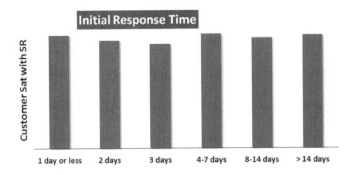

Figure 28.2. Relationship between initial response time and customer satisfaction with SR

Using Number of Ownership Changes, Oracle found that customers were more satisfied with their SRs that had fewer ownership changes compared to customers whose SRs had more ownership changes (See Figure 28.3.).

Figure 28.3. Relationship between number of SR ownership changes and customer satisfaction with SR

The application of Big Data solutions at Oracle has provided much insight regarding how the management of customers through the Service Request process can be facilitated with the use of operational metrics. The analyses showed that not all operational metrics are predictive of customer satisfaction; *initial response time was unrelated to customer satisfaction*, suggesting that monitoring metrics associated with that aspect of the SR process is unnecessary in improving customer satisfaction. To improve the customer experience with the SR process (e.g., improve customer satisfaction), changes to the SR process are best directed at elements of the SR process that will impact the *resolution time* and the *number of ownership changes*.

Summary

Linking disparate data silos proved useful for Oracle. They were able to identify the operational metrics that were important to customers. More importantly, they were able to identify operational metrics that were not important to driving customer satisfaction.

Proper application of Big Data principles helps expand the types of metrics you can use as part of your customer experience strategy. By taking a customer-centric approach in their analyses of their Big Data, Oracle was able to link operational metrics to customer feedback metrics to identify how the operational metrics are related to customer satisfaction. This type of approach to understanding all your business data will help you build customer-centric operational metrics, manage customer relationships using operational metrics and reward employees based on operational metrics that matter to the customer.

Chapter 29: The Importance of Customer Experience is Overinflated

"It is common sense to take a method and try it. If it fails, admit it frankly and try another. But above all, try something."

Franklin D. Roosevelt

Customer experience management programs require measurement of primarily two types of variables, satisfaction with the customer experience and customer loyalty. These metrics are used specifically to assess the importance of customer experience in improving customer loyalty. Determining the "importance" of different customer experience attributes needs to be precise as it plays a major role in helping companies: 1) prioritize improvement efforts, 2) estimate return on investment (ROI) of improvement efforts and 3) allocate company resources.

How We Determine Importance of Customer Experience Attributes

When we label a customer experience attribute as "important," we typically are referring to the magnitude of the correlation between customer ratings on that attribute (e.g., product quality, account management, customer service) and a measure of customer loyalty (e.g., recommend, renew service contract). Correlations can vary from 0.0 to 1.0. Those attributes that have a high correlation with customer loyalty (approaching 1.0) are considered more "important" than other attributes that have a low correlation with customer loyalty (approaching 0.0).

Measuring Satisfaction with the Customer Experience and Customer Loyalty via Surveys

Companies typically (almost always?) rely on customer surveys to measure both the satisfaction with the customer experience (CX) as well as the level of customer loyalty. That is, customers are given a survey that includes questions about the customer experience and customer loyalty. The customers are asked to make ratings about their satisfaction with the customer experience and their level of customer loyalty (typically likelihood ratings).

As mentioned earlier, to identify the importance of customer experience attributes on customer loyalty, ratings of CX metrics and customer loyalty are correlated with each other.

The Problem of a Single Method of Measurement: Common Method Variance

The magnitude of the correlations between measures of satisfaction (with the customer experience) and measures of customer loyalty are made up of different components. On one hand, the correlation is due to the "true" relationship between satisfaction with the experience and customer loyalty.

On the other hand, because the two variables are measured using the **same method - a survey with self-reported ratings)**, the magnitude of the correlation is partly due to the method of how the data are collected. Referred to as Common Method Variance (CMV) and studied in the field of social sciences (see Campbell and Fiske, 1959) where surveys are a common method of data collection, the general finding is that the correlation between two different measures is driven partly by the true relationship between the constructs being measured as well as **the way they are measured**.

The impact of CMV in customer experience management likely occurs when you use the same method of collecting data (e.g., survey questions) for both predictors (e.g., satisfaction with the customer experience) and outcomes (e.g., customer loyalty). That is, the size of the correlation between satisfaction and loyalty metrics is **likely due to the fact that both variables are measured using a survey instrument.**

Customer Loyalty Measures: Real Behaviors v. Expected Behaviors

The CMV problem is not really about how we measure satisfaction with the customer experience; a survey is a good way to measure the feelings/perceptions behind the customers' experience. The problem lies with how we measure customer loyalty. Customer loyalty is about actual customer behavior. It is real customer behavior (e.g., number of recommendations, number of products purchased, whether a customer renewed their service contract) that drives company profits. Popular self-report measures ask for customers' estimation of their likelihood of engaging in certain behaviors in the future (e.g., likely to recommend, likely to purchase, likely to renew).

Using self-report measures of satisfaction and loyalty, researchers have found high correlations between these two variables; For example, Bruce Temkin has found correlations between satisfaction with the customer experience and NPS to be around .70. Similarly, in my research, I have found comparably sized correlations ($r \approx$ .50) looking at the impact of the customer experience on advocacy loyalty (the recommend question is part of my advocacy metric). Are these correlations a good reflection of the importance of the customer experience in predicting loyalty (as measured by the recommend question)? Before I answer that question, let us first look at work (Sharma, Yetton and Crawford, 2009) that helps us classify different types of customer measurement and their impact on correlations.

Different Ways to Measure Customer Loyalty

Sharma et al. highlight four different types of measurement methods. I have slightly modified their four types to illustrate customer loyalty measures that are least susceptible to CMV (coded as 1) to measures that are most susceptible to CMV (coded as 4):

- **System-captured metrics reflect objective metrics of customer loyalty:** Data are obtained from historical records and other objective sources, including purchase records (captured in a CRM system). Example: Computer generated records of "time spent on the Web site" or "number of products/services purchased" or "whether a customer renewed their service contract."

- **Behavioral-continuous items reflect specific loyalty behaviors**

273

that respondents have carried out: Responses are typically captured on a continuous scale. Example item: How many friends did you tell about company XYZ in the past 12 months? None to 10, say.

- **Behaviorally-anchored items reflect specific actions that respondents have carried out:** Responses are typically captured on scales with behavioral anchors. Example item: How often have you shopped at store XYZ in the past month? Not at all to Very Often.

- **Perceptually-anchored items reflect perceptions of loyalty behavior:** Responses are typically on Likert scales, semantic differential or "agree/disagree scale". Example: I shop at the store regularly. Agree to Disagree.

These researchers looked at 75 different studies examining the correlation between perceived usefulness (predictor) and usage of IT (criterion). While all studies used perceptually-anchored measures for perceived usefulness (**perception/attitude**), different studies used one of four different types of measures of usage (**behavior**). These researchers found that CMV accounted for 59% of the variance in the relationship between perceived usefulness and usage (r = .59 for perceptually-anchored items; r = .42 for behaviorally anchored items; r = .29 for behavioral continuous items; r = .16 for system-captured metrics). That is, the method with which researchers measure "usage" impacts the outcome of the results; as the usage measures become less susceptible to CMV (moving up the scale from 4 to 1 above), the magnitude of the correlation decreases between perceived usefulness and usage.

Looking at research in the CEM space, we commonly see that customer loyalty is measured using questions that reflect perceptually-anchored questions (type 4 above), the type of measure most susceptible to CMV.

An Example

I have some survey data on the wireless service industry that examined the impact of customer satisfaction with customer touch points (e.g., product, coverage/reliability and customer service) on customer loyalty. This study included measures of satisfaction with the customer experience (perceptually-anchored) and two different measures of customer loyalty:

- Self-reported number of people you recommended the company to in the past 12 months (behavioral-continuous).

- Self-reported likelihood to recommend (perceptually-anchored)

	Mean	SD	N	1	2	3	4	5
1 Number of friends/colleagues*	5.75	4.30	5012	--				
2 Likelihood to recommend	6.78	2.58	5367	.47	--			
3 Product/Service Quality	3.63	.89	5088	.38	.63	(.79)		
4 Coverage/Reliability	3.81	.98	5060	.22	.46	.57	(.70)	
5 Customer Service	3.44	.97	5054	.24	.46	.59	.43	(.90)

Source: Wireless service provider: Survey of 5686 global consumers from 2010. Mob4Hire

* Number of friend/colleagues measured by question: How many friends/colleagues have you recommended your wireless service provider to in the past 12 months (none to 10+)
Likelihood to recommend measured by question: How likely are you to recommend your wireless service provider to friends/colleagues (0 - Not at all likely to 10 - Extremely likely)
Customer experience (CX) with touchpoints are averaged measures assesed by questions: 1) Product/Service Quality - products are excellent, service is excellent; 2) Coverage/Reliability - good coverage in my area, has reliable service (e.g., few dropped calls); and 3) Customer Service - reps respond timely, reps knowledgable, reps courteous, reps understand needs, reps always there. Each of these CX questions use the scale: 1 - Strongly Disagree to 5 - Strongly Agree.
Reliability estimates (Cronbach's alpha) for composite scores are located in the diagonal (in italics).

Table 29.1. Descriptive statistics and correlations of two types of recommend loyalty metrics (behavioral-continuous and perceptually-anchored) with customer experience ratings.

The correlations among these measures are located in Table 29.1. As you can see, the two recommend loyalty metrics are weakly related to each other ($r = .47$), suggesting that they measure two different constructs. Additionally, and as expected by the CMV model, the behavioral-continuous measure of customer loyalty (number of friends/colleagues) shows a significantly lower correlation (average $r = .28$) with customer experience ratings compared to the perceptually-anchored measure of customer loyalty (likelihood to recommend) (average $r = .52$). These findings are strikingly similar to the above findings of Sharma et al. (2009).

Summary and Implications

The way in which we measure the customer experience and customer loyalty impacts the correlations we see between them. Because measures of both variables use perceptually-anchored questions, the **correlation between the two is likely overinflated**. I contend that the true impact of customer experience on customer loyalty can only be determined when real customer loyalty behaviors are used in the statistical modeling process.

We may be overestimating the importance (e.g., impact) of customer experience on customer loyalty simply due to the fact that we measure both variables (experience and loyalty) using the same instrument, a survey with similar scale characteristics. Companies commonly use the correlations (or squared correlation) between a given attribute and customer loyalty as the basis for estimating the return on investment (ROI) when improving the customer experience. The use of overinflated correlations will likely result in an overestimate of the ROI of customer experience improvement efforts. As such, companies need to temper this estimation when perceptually-anchored customer loyalty metrics are used.

To combat the problem of CMV, companies need to use more objective metrics of customer loyalty whenever they are available. While measuring customer loyalty using real, objective metrics (system-captured) would be ideal, many companies do not have the resources to collect and link customer loyalty behaviors to customer ratings of their experience. Perhaps loyalty measures that are less susceptible to CMV could be developed and used to get a more realistic assessment of the importance of the customer experience on customer loyalty. For example, self-reported metrics that are more easily verifiable by the company (e.g., "likelihood to renew service contract" is more easily verifiable by the company than "likelihood to recommend") might encourage customers to provide realistic ratings about their expected behaviors, thus reflecting a truer measure of customer loyalty.

The impact of the Common Method Variance in CEM research is likely strong in studies in which the data for customer satisfaction (the predictor) and customer loyalty (the criterion) are collected using surveys with similar item characteristics (perceptually-anchored). You need to keep the problem of CMV in mind when interpreting customer survey results (any survey results, really) and estimating the impact of customer experience on customer loyalty.

Section 6: Extra

"You're damned if you do and damned if you don't."

Bart Simpson

The last section of the book is dedicated to a few miscellaneous topics that are important to the field of customer experience management. In this section, I show you that, in addition to service quality, product quality is still an important determinant of customer loyalty. Also, I will address how startups can gain value from the research in CEM program and propose how they can bootstrap their way to incorporating CEM practices early in their history. Also, I will take a look at the state of the patient experience for US hospitals using publicly available data on patient satisfaction from the federal government. The Affordable Care Act I apply analytics (those that I introduced earlier in the book) to show what US hospitals need to do to improve patient loyalty. The field of CEM is fraught with misinformation; to help combat this problem, I provide tips on how you can change people's beliefs.

To illustrate the best practices that I outlined in this book, I present an in-depth look at Oracle's CEM program along with some of the benefits that they have experienced as a result of their best practices. Finally, I leave you with a free online self-assessment for you to complete. The results of this brief assessment will show you how your company's CEM program stacks up against best practices.

Chapter 30: Don't Forget about Product Quality

"Sure what we do has to make commercial sense, but it's never the starting point. We start with the product and the user experience."

Steve Jobs

My daughter and I visited the Apple store in downtown San Francisco to take a peek at their new iPad 3 (released the prior week). Of course, the store was packed full of Apple fans, each trying out the new iPad. This particular in-store experience got me thinking about the role of product vs. customer service/tech support in driving customer loyalty to a brand or company.

Product vs. Tech Support

There has been much talk about how companies need to focus on customer service/tech support to help differentiate themselves from their competitors. While I believe that customer service/tech support is important in improving the customer relationship to increase customer loyalty, this focus on customer service has distracted attention from the importance of the product.

I will illustrate my point using some data on PC manufacturers I collected a few years ago. I have three variables for this analysis:

- Advocacy Loyalty

- PC Quality

- Tech Support Quality

Advocacy Loyalty was measured using 4 items (e.g., overall sat, recommend, buy again, and choose again for first time) using a 0 to 10 scale. PC Quality and Tech Support Quality were each measured on a 1 (Strongly Disagree) to 5 (Strongly Agree) scale. PC Quality was the average of three questions (PC meets expectations, PC is reliable, PC has features I want). Tech Support Quality was the average of six questions (tech support timely, knowledgeable, courteous, understands needs, always there when needed).

Product is More Important than Technical Support in Driving Advocacy Loyalty

The descriptive statistics and correlations among these variables are located in Table 30.1. A path diagram of these variables is presented in Figure 30.1. As you can see, when comparing the impact of each of the customer touch points on advocacy loyalty, PC quality has the largest impact (.68) while Tech Support as the smallest impact (.21) on advocacy loyalty.

	Mean	SD	N	Variables		
				1	2	3
1 Advocacy Loyalty Index	7.57	2.22	717	(.94)	.68	.22
2 PC Quality	4.08	.79	717	.79	(.88)	.29
3 Technical Support Quality	3.66	.90	717	.59	.62	(.96)

Bivariate correlations are located in the lower half of the correlation matrix. Partial correlations (controlling for the effect of the third variable) are located in the upper half of the correlation matrix. Reliability estimates (Cronbach's alpha) for each measure are located in the diagonal.

Source: Data from Hayes, B.E. (2011). Lessons in loyalty. Quality Progress, March, 24-31.
Sample of about 1000 adult US respondents surveyed in July 2007 about their personal computer manufacturer.

PCs with ample sample size were included in the analysis. Respondents who indicated Apple as their PC manufacturer were omitted because their responses were extremely high and would skew the results.

Path coefficients are the partial correlations between the two variables, controlling for the third variable.

Table 30.1. Descriptive Statistics and Correlations among Variables

As the results show, advocacy loyalty is more highly correlated with PC quality (.79) than with technical support quality (.59). After controlling for the effect of the other attribute, PC quality is much more closely linked to advocacy loyalty (.68) than technical support quality (.22).

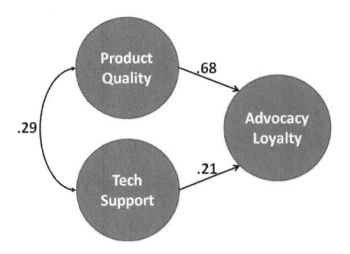

Source: Data from Hayes, B.E. (2011). Lessons in loyalty. Quality Progress, March, 24-31.
Sample of about 1000 adult US respondents surveyed in July 2007 about their personal computer manufacturer.

PCs with ample sample size were included in the analysis. Respondents who indicated Apple as their PC manufacturer were omitted because their responses were extremely high and would skew the results.

Path coefficients are the partial correlations between the two variables, controlling for the third variable.

Figure 30.1. Path Diagram of Study Variables

Summary

People don't frequent a store primarily because of the service. They flock to a company because of the primary product the company provides. Can we please temper all this talk about how important service quality is relative to the product? Ask anybody at that Apple store why they were there and they would tell you it was because of the products, not the service.

284

Chapter 31: Three CEM Tips for Startups

"With data collection, 'the sooner the better' is always the best answer."

Marissa Mayer

Founders of startup companies have limited resources. Coupled with plenty on their plates, founders appear to be unable to invest in programs that support processes outside of standard business practices (e.g., marketing, sales and services). They are responsible for every aspect of the company, from raising capital and creating products to implementing a marketing plan to providing support. There often is very little time/resources to devote to a formal CEM program.

A growing startup, however, can still implement key CEM best practices in a cost-effective way. Below are three things startups can do to integrate the voice of the customer in their business processes and begin to build a formal CEM program.

1. Start with the Executives

A good first place to start your CEM journey is at the top of your organization. Through their actions and established policies, top executives set the tone and culture of the company. Without their support, the success of any program is likely to fail. We know that companies who have executive support around the CEM program have greater success (e.g., higher customer loyalty, higher satisfaction with their CEM program) compared to companies with little/no executive support.

Here are a few things start-ups can do to improve executive-level support:

- **Incorporate a customer-focus in the vision/mission statement**. Support the company mission by presenting customer-related information (e.g., customer satisfaction/loyalty goals) in the employee handbook. Use customer feedback metrics to set and monitor company goals.

- **Identify an executive as the champion of the CEM program**. A senior level executive "owns" the CEM program and reports customer feedback results at executive meetings. Senior executives evangelize the CEM program in their communication with employees and customers. Senior executives receive training on the CEM program.

- **Use customer feedback in decision-making process**. Include customer metrics in company's balanced scorecard along with other, traditional scorecard metrics. This practice will ensure executives and employees understand the importance of these metrics and are aware of current levels of customer satisfaction/loyalty. Present customer feedback results in company meetings and official documents.

2. Collect Customer Feedback

You cannot manage what you do not measure. These words ring true for your CEM program. Loyalty leaders collect customer feedback using a variety of sources (surveys, social media, and brand communities). When you collect customer feedback, you need to consider what you measure and how you collect the feedback.

Here are a few things start-ups can do around collecting customer feedback.

- **Conduct an annual / bi-annual customer survey.** While loyalty leaders collect customer feedback using a variety of sources (e.g., relationship survey, transactional survey, web survey social media), a good start would be to start with a relationship survey conducted annually/bi-annually.

- **Measure different types of customer loyalty.** Selecting the right mix of customer loyalty questions will ensure you can grow your business through new and existing customers. Determine the important customer loyalty behaviors (retention, advocacy, purchasing) and measure them.

- **Use automated (e.g., Web) tools to collect and report customer feedback metrics.** Web tools not only facilitate data collection, but with the ever-increasing adoption of a Web lifestyle, they are also becoming a necessity. Data collection via the Web is cost-effective, allows for quick integration with other data sources and speeds reporting of customer feedback. There are several free survey services you can use to start collecting customer feedback: SurveyMonkey, Zoomerang. While these free services provide reports, they do not allow you access to the raw data. Also, you might consider using Limesurvey, an open-source, enterprise-quality survey engine; Limesurvey allows you to access your raw survey data.

In addition to providing insights about how best to manage your customers, customer feedback can help startups in a variety of ways:

- **Improving ROI:** Resources are tight for startups. Startups that spend their resources wisely will outperform those who do not. Customer surveys (and accompanying analysis) can help you understand where you need to make improvements (e.g., make investments) that will improve customer loyalty.

- **Beating your competition**: Knowing where your brand sits in the competitive landscape impacts your growth. Top tier companies have customers who are more willing to buy more from them compared to bottom tier companies. Collecting customer feedback can help you identify what you need to do to beat your competition and improve your growth.

- **Acquiring capital investments**: Investors use a lot of different information to identify investment potentials. Set yourself apart from other startups seeking money buy providing investment professionals the information about the quality of your customer relationships. Collecting customer feedback and using customer feedback metrics (e.g., customer loyalty) can help you estimate the monetary value of your startup. Help investors understand the quality of your relationship with your customers.

3. Share Feedback Results Company-wide

A good way to build your startup around your customers is to share the results of your customer survey with the employees.

- **Share CEM program results throughout the company**. Use Web-based reporting tools to allow easy access to the results by all employees. Regularly publish customer feedback results to all employees via emails/reports.

- **Use simple statistics to convey results and try to incorporate something visually interesting about the results**. Avoid sharing complex results with employees that might confuse them rather than educate them. Use simple statistics like means and frequencies. Avoid using difference scores (e.g., commonly called net scores) as they are ambiguous and unnecessary. Consider using visually stunning ways to present your data. A visually stunning presentation of the data, compared to bar graphs, will more likely be examined by the consumers of your reports.

Summary

Startups, to succeed, need to build a company that encourages customers to recommend their brand, buy more from them (as startups expand their product line / service offerings) and remain as a long-term customer. How can startups implement a CEM program? Based on best practices research in CEM, I offer three suggestions on how startups can begin incorporating customer feedback into their DNA.

Startups can begin by **educating the leaders on the importance of the customer experience and customer loyalty to business success**. The outcome of this education process is designed to instill a sense of importance of the customer in the mindset of the senior management team. **Startups can easily collect customer feedback through an annual/bi-annual survey**. This survey needs to focus on measuring these key areas about your customer: 1) customer loyalty, 2) customer experience, 3) how they view you relative to the competition and 4) company-specific questions. **Finally, startups need to communicate the results of the customer feedback to the entire company**. Sharing customer feedback company-wide lets employees know that senior management conveys the importance of the customer throughout the company.

The formation of a CEM program early in your company's history helps build a culture that is focused around the customer. Having a formal CEM program lets potential job candidates understand the importance of the customer and helps create a culture that is focused around the customer. As your company grows, your CEM program will mature and expand, incorporating other ways of collecting customer feedback (e.g., transaction surveys, social media) as well as other sources of business data to help you build a solid customer research program.

Chapter 32: Patient Experience in US Hospitals

"Hiding within those mounds of data is knowledge that could change the life of a patient, or change the world."

Atul Butte

The U.S. government provides a variety of publicly available databases that include metrics on the performance of US hospitals, including patient experience (PX) database, health outcome database, process of care database and medical spending database. I applied CEM principles (e.g., primarily analytics) found in this book along with Big Data principles (e.g., integration of different metrics from their respective databases) to these data sources to better understand the quality of US hospitals and determine ways they can improve the patient experience and the overall healthcare delivery system. I spent the summer of 2012 analyzing these data, and am summarizing the major findings here.

Why the Patient Experience (PX) has Become an

Important Topic for U.S. Hospitals

The Centers for Medicare & Medicaid Services (CMS) will be using patient feedback about their care as part of their reimbursement plan for acute care hospitals. The purpose of the VBP program is to promote better clinical outcomes for patients and improve their experience of care during hospital stays. Not surprisingly, hospitals are focusing on improving the patient experience to ensure they receive the maximum of their incentive payments.

Key Findings from Analyses of Big Data of US Hospitals

Hospitals, like all big businesses, struggle with knowing "if you do this, then you will succeed with this." While hospital administrators can rely on gut feelings, intuition and anecdotal evidence to guide their decisions on how to improve their hospitals, data-driven decision-making provides better, more reliable, insights about real things hospital administrators can do to improve their hospitals. While interpretation of my analyses of these Big Data is debatable, the data are what they are.

I have highlighted some key findings below that provide value for different constituencies: 1) healthcare consumers can find the best hospitals, 2) healthcare providers can focus on areas that improve how they deliver healthcare, and 3) healthcare researchers can uncover deeper insights about factors that impact the patient experience and health outcomes.

The Survey of Patients' Hospital Experience

This survey is known as HCAHPS (Hospital Consumer Assessment of Healthcare Providers and Systems). HCAHPS (pronounced *"H-caps"*) is a national, standardized survey of hospital patients and was developed by a partnership of public and private organizations.

The development of HCAHPS was funded by the Federal government, specifically the Centers for Medicare & Medicade Services (CMS) and the Agency for Healthcare Research and Quality (AHRQ). HCAHPS was created to publicly report the patient's perspective of hospital care.

The Data

The data I used for the current analysis were updated in 5/30/2012. Based on HCAHPS reporting schedule, it appears the current survey data were collected from Q3 2010 through Q2 2011 and represented the latest publicly available patient survey data at the time of my analyses.

The survey asks a random sample of recently discharged patients about important aspects of their hospital experience. The data set includes patient survey results for over 3800 US hospitals on ten measures of patients' perspectives of care. The 10 measures are:

1. Nurses communicate well

5. Doctors communicate well

6. Received help as soon as they wanted (Responsive)

7. Pain well controlled

8. Staff explain medicines before giving to patients

9. Room and bathroom are clean

10. Area around room is quiet at night

11. Given information about what to do during recovery at home

12. Overall hospital rating

13. Recommend hospital to friends and family (Recommend)

For questions 1 through 7, respondents were asked to provide frequency ratings about the occurrence of each attribute (Never, Sometimes, Usually, Always). For question 8, respondents were provided a Y/N option. For question 9, respondents were asked to provide an overall rating of the hospital on a scale from 0 (Worst hospital possible) to 10 (Best hospital possible). For question 10, respondents were asked to provide their likelihood of recommending the hospital (Definitely no, Probably no, Probably yes, Definitely yes).

The Metrics

The data set reported metrics for each hospital as percentages of responses. Because the data set had already been somewhat aggregated (e.g., percentages reported for group of response options), I was unable to calculate average scores for each hospital. Instead, I used top box scores as the metric of patient experience. I found that top box scores are highly correlated with average scores, suggesting that these two metrics tell us the same thing about the companies (in our case, hospitals).

Top box scores for the respective rating scales are defined as: 1) Percent of patients who reported "Always"; 2) Percent of patients who reported "Yes"; 3) Percent of patients who gave a rating of 9 or 10; 4) Percent of patients who said "Definitely yes."

Top box scores provide an easy-to-understand way of communicating the survey results for different types of scales. Even though there are four different rating scales for the survey questions, using a top box reporting method puts all metrics on the same numeric scale. **Across all 10 metrics, hospital scores can range from 0 (bad) to 100 (good).**

Results

The descriptive statistics of and correlations among the metrics are located in Table 32.1. As you can see in the table, all correlations among the metrics are statistically significant, indicating that hospitals tend to receive consistent ratings across different metrics; that is, some hospitals tend to get high ratings across all metrics and other hospitals tend to get low ratings across all metrics.

		Percent Top Box	SD	N	Correlations Among Patient Experience Metrics									
					1	2	3	4	5	6	7	8	9	10
1	Nurses communicate well	76.55	6.03	3851	--									
2	Doctors communicate well	80.44	5.51	3851	0.77	--								
3	Responsive	64.55	9.25	3851	0.86	0.72	--							
4	Pain well controlled	69.52	5.78	3851	0.82	0.68	0.75	--						
5	Staff explains medicines	61.23	6.76	3847	0.80	0.70	0.77	0.73	--					
6	Room and bathroom are clean	71.74	7.65	3851	0.72	0.57	0.74	0.60	0.63	--				
7	Area around room quiet at night	58.68	10.54	3851	0.63	0.63	0.63	0.56	0.60	0.53	--			
8	Given information about my recovery	82.72	4.93	3850	0.52	0.36	0.44	0.43	0.47	0.38	0.24	--		
9	Overall hospital quality rating	88.07	9.17	3851	0.80	0.62	0.70	0.72	0.67	0.65	0.56	0.58	--	
10	Recommend hospital	69.74	10.08	3851	0.67	0.48	0.54	0.60	0.55	0.50	0.41	0.55	0.90	--

Note: Data are from HCAHPS patient survey data from Q3 2010 through Q2 2011, the latest publicly available patient survey data from HCAHPS. Data were downloaded between June 1 through June 10, 2012. For more information on the data, go here: https://explore.data.gov/Health-and-Nutrition/CMS-Federated-Datasets/r2ab-jrvf

Table 32.1. Descriptive statistics of and correlations among patient experience metrics.

State of Patient Experience from Hospital's Perspective

The Beryl Institutde and Catalyst Healthcare Research conducted a 2011 benchmarking study to understand what hospitals are doing to improve the patient experience (I recommend you read the study report.). This study collected responses from 790 respondents (representing

660 individual hospitals or hospital groups/systems).

The researchers found that (see Figure 32.1) respondents said their organization's top 3 priorities to improve the patient experience are (in descending order of importance):

1. Reduce Noise

2. Patient Rounding

3. Discharge Process and Instructions

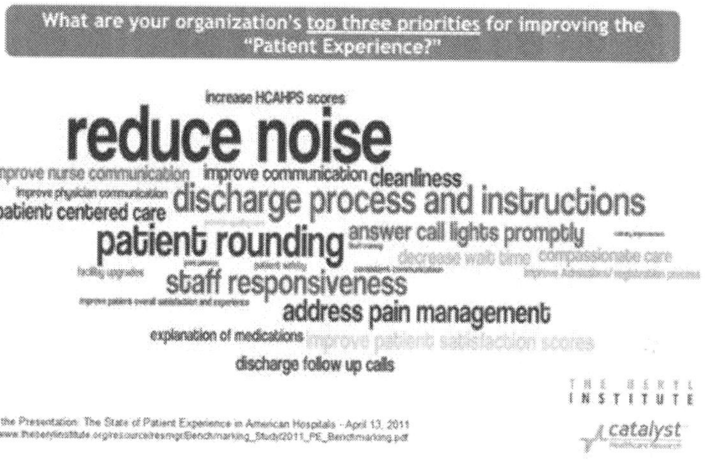

Figure 32.1. State of Patient Experience in American Hospitals. Figure is from a 2011 study by The Beryl Institute and Catalyst Healthcare Research. The research summary can be found here.

Are those the right PX areas in which hospitals should be focused if they want to optimize the value of their PX improvement efforts? Let's take a look from the patient's perspective. Here is one way to prioritize PX improvements.

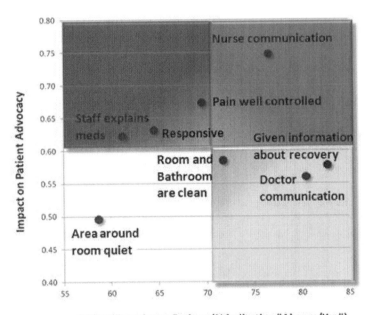

Figure 32.2. Loyalty Driver Matrix for Patient Survey

Loyalty Driver Analysis

The driver matrix using the patient survey data

appear in Figure 32.2. We see that there are three key drivers of patient advocacy: 1) Staff explains meds, 2) Responsiveness and 3) Pain well controlled. These areas appear in the upper left quadrant and suggest that these areas are important to patient advocacy **and** have much room for improvement.

State of Patient Experience from Patient's Perspective

Results showed that, of the 8 PX areas being measured by HCAHPS - and used for CMS reimbursements (see Table 32.2), the three PX areas that received the lowest ratings (possible scores can range from 0 to 100) are:

- Area around room quiet (~58)

- Staff explains medicines before dispensing (~60)

- Staff responsiveness (~63)

It appears that hospital improvements in reducing noise parallels patients' low ratings in that exact area. Additionally, improvement of patient rounding might improve patient satisfaction with responsiveness. However, even though hospitals' are focusing on process discharge and instructions, this PX area receives the highest rating (~82) of the 8 PX areas in the HCAHPS. Note: The correlations among the HCAHPS 10 questions show roughly the same relative pattern whether the data are analyzed at the hospital level or patient level.

Acute Care Hospitals

		Percent Top Box	SD	N	Correlations Among Patient Experience Metrics								
					1	2	3	4	5	6	7	8	9
1	Patient Advocacy Index	68.31	9.44	3318	.95								
2	Nurses communicate well	75.83	5.92	3318	0.75	--							
3	Doctors communicate well	79.77	5.32	3318	0.55	0.76	--						
4	Responsive	63.06	8.70	3318	0.64	0.86	0.71	--					
5	Pain well controlled	69.07	5.66	3318	0.69	0.84	0.69	0.78	--				
6	Staff explains medicines	60.40	6.34	3316	0.64	0.82	0.70	0.78	0.76	--			
7	Room and bathroom are clean	70.52	7.08	3318	0.58	0.71	0.54	0.72	0.63	0.63	--		
8	Area around room quiet at night	57.92	10.60	3318	0.49	0.62	0.64	0.65	0.57	0.63	0.52	--	
9	Given information about my recovery	82.40	4.80	3317	0.60	0.53	0.34	0.44	0.43	0.48	0.38	0.23	--

Cronbach's alpha (reliability estimate) is located in the diagonal. No reliability estimates are calculated for single-item scales.

Note: Data are from HCAHPS patient survey data from Q3 2010 through Q2 2011, the latest publicly available patient survey data from HCAHPS. Data were downloaded between June 1 through June 10, 2012. For more information on the data, go here: https://explore.data.gov/Health-and-Nutrition/CMS-Federated-Datasets/r2ab-jrvf

Table 32.2. Descriptive statistics of and correlations among PX areas and patient loyalty for Acute Care hospitals.

Setting Priorities for Improving the Patient Experience

One thing struck me about the Beryl Institute findings; different hospitals focus on different things as their top priorities. I would be very interested to learn *how hospitals prioritize* improvements in patient experience. Why did some hospitals focus on noise reduction and others focus on nurse communication or cleanliness? What organizational factors did hospital executives weigh when prioritizing their investment dollars? Did they use patient experience data? If so, how did they use patient experience data to arrive at their improvement decisions?

The CMS reimbursement incentive plan might

encourage hospital executives to look solely at ways to maximize/increase PX ratings with a limited budget. While improving patient experience is a positive outcome for the hospital in and of itself (100% reimbursement), you need to consider PX improvements' long-term impact on outcomes like patient loyalty.

Medical Spending and Patient Satisfaction

Medicare tracks how much they spend on each patient with Medicare who is admitted to a hospital compared to the amount Medicare spends per hospital patient nationally. Also known as "Medicare Spending per Beneficiary_(MSPB)", this measure assesses the cost of care. By measuring cost of care with this measure, CMS hopes to increase the transparency of care for consumers and recognize hospitals that are involved in the provision of high-quality care at lower cost to Medicare.

The MSPB measure for each hospital is calculated as the ratio of the MSPB Amount for the hospital divided by the median MSPB Amount across all hospitals. A hospital with an MSPB value of 1.0 indicates that the hospital's spending per patient is average. A hospital with an MSPB value less than 1.0 indicates that the hospital's spending per patient is less than the average hospital. A hospital with an MSPB value greater than 1.0 indicates that the hospital's spending per patient is greater than the average hospital.

Medicare Spend is not Related to Patient Loyalty/Experience

Hospitals were divided into 10 groups based on their MSPB score. Figure 32.3 contains the plot of patient advocacy for each of the 10 MSPB levels. Figure 32.4 contains the plot of patient experience ratings for each of the 10 MSPB levels.

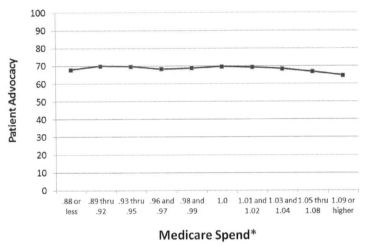

* Also known as "Medicare Spending per Beneficiary", this measure shows information about how much Medicare spends on each person with Medicare who is admitted to a hospital compared to the amount Medicare spends per hospital patient nationally.

Note: Data are from HCAHPS patient survey data from Q3 2010 through Q2 2011.
For more information on the data, go here:
https://explore.data.gov/Health-and-Nutrition/CMS-Federated-Datasets/r2ab-jrvf

Figure 32.3. Patient Loyalty by Medicare Spending per Beneficiary.

There were statistically significant differences across the 10 segments. Although these differences were statistically significant, the differences were not substantial. Specifically, the MSPB segments accounted for about 4.5% of the variance in patient metrics.

We might expect hospitals that spend more on medical services per patient would receive higher patient experience ratings. The patients are, after all, receiving more resources directed toward them compared to hospitals that spend less on medical services. If anything, we see that as the cost of care goes up, patient experience actually decreases (however slightly).

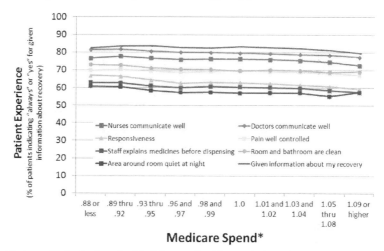

Figure 32.4. Patient Experience by Medicare Spending per Beneficiary

Summary

The value of insights gained from combining, integrating

disparate databases (especially ones including both attitudinal and operational/objective metrics) provide much greater value than any single database can provide by itself. That is one of the major values of using Big Data principles. The integrated health care Big Data set provided rich in insights and allowed us to answer bigger questions about how to best improve the patient experience and health outcomes.

There are a few important points we can conclude based on the analyses of patient experience ratings:

- **The biggest driver of patient advocacy is the patients' perception of the quality of nurses' communication effectiveness**. Because nurses are likely involved with most of the day-to-day dealings with patient care, their performance impacts many different facets of the patient experience (e.g., Responsiveness, staff explains med).

- **To improve patient loyalty toward hospitals, the hospital industry might consider focusing on three areas: 1) Pain management, 2) Responsiveness and 3) Staff explaining meds to patients**. As an industry, these three patient experience areas appear as key drivers of patient loyalty; that is, each has much room for improvement and has a relatively big impact on patient advocacy.

• **The quality of doctor communication is the second lowest driver of patient advocacy**. While doctor communication quality is still important to patient advocacy (r = .56 with patient advocacy), it is less important than other patient experience areas like cleanliness of the patients' rooms, responsiveness (getting help when needed), and getting information about their home recovery. Doctors' involvement might be perceived as less important to the patients simply because the patients have less exposure to doctors, especially when compared to the patient's exposure to nurses.

• **Patient Advocacy Index (PAI) appears to be a reliable, valid metric of patient loyalty**. This two-item scale has high reliability and is related logically to other patient experience metrics. While the PAI is a good metric of patient advocacy, the hospital industry might consider examining other types of ways that patients can demonstrate their loyalty toward their hospital. In my research, I have found that there are three general types of customer loyalty (e.g., advocacy, purchasing and retention), each responsible for different types of business outcomes. Perhaps hospitals need to expand their idea regarding patient loyalty and develop measures that reliably tap different ways patients can show their loyalty towards hospitals.

- **Hospitals' improvement priorities do not seem to match up with what patients want.** Hospital executives' top priorities for improving the patient experience are: 1) Reduce Noise, 2) Patient Rounding and 3) Discharge Process and Instructions. Patients, however, say they are least satisfied with the following areas: 1) Area around room quiet, 2) Staff explains medicines before dispensing and 3) Staff responsiveness.

- **Hospitals with lower medical spend per patient are able to deliver a comparable patient experience to hospitals with greater medical spend per patient**. It appears that the amount of money a hospital spends directly on patient care has no impact on the patients' experience. It would be interesting to determine how other types of hospital spending – better TVs for patients, better facilities for families - impacts the patient experience.

Hospital executives are tasked with improving the patient experience. Their priorities are driven by short-term monetary metrics (e.g., CMS reimbursement) and long-term hospital growth metrics (e.g., patient loyalty). Hospital executives can use their hospital's PX survey data (e.g., HCAHPS) to help priorities PX improvement opportunities to maximize both metrics to optimize the ROI of their decision.

Patient loyalty is only one of many different outcomes a hospital can use to prioritize their improvements around the patient experience. Executives can even look at how patient experience is related to other outcome metrics like hospital mortality rates and readmission rates to understand how their PX improvement dollars improve different types of key hospital outcomes.

Chapter 33: Battling Misinformation

"You can't be distracted by the noise of misinformation"

James Daly

I read an article in Scientific American that has implications about the field of customer experience management (CEM). The researchers discuss the phenomenon of widely held beliefs that are not true. Think about President Barack Obama's US citizenship status still being questioned even though he has released his birth certificate and his birth in Hawaii has been corroborated by the news media. Despite these facts, 51% of voters in the 2011 Republican primary election believed Obama was born abroad.

Phenomena that are even supported by sound, scientific evidence are not immune to misinformation. Think about people who believe that global warming is not caused by humans. Think about people who believe that vaccines cause autism. Even our own elected officials believe that women have magical vaginas capable of preventing pregnancies in cases of "legitimate" rape

(Google Todd Akin) and that the earth is only 9000 years old (Google Rep. Paul Brown). Despite the preponderance of scientific evidence to the contrary, people still hold these beliefs.

Misinformation in Customer Experience Management

I feel that the misinformation machine is going strong in the field of CEM. I have written about CEM practices that are good examples of unsubstantiated beliefs: 1) measuring employee engagement is key to driving better business outcomes (e.g., higher customer loyalty, increased employee performance, business growth) and 2) the Net Promoter Score (NPS) is the best predictor of business growth (better than satisfaction and other loyalty questions).

In my research, however, I found little support for these claims. Specifically, most measures of employee engagement are only relabeled measures of employee satisfaction. So, researchers using these questionable "employee engagement" measures are really studying the phenomenon of employee satisfaction, not employee engagement; thus, attributing growth to employee engagement is not warranted. With respect to the misinformation about the NPS, I and others have found that other questions of customer loyalty are equally good as the NPS in predicting business growth; also, different types of loyalty questions predict different types of business growth.

While these CEM-related examples have much less significance to the general public, they still represent beliefs that, I think, impede progress in our field, both practical and theoretical. Even though the CEM misinformation machine is not necessarily driven by dishonest people, the lack of dishonestly does not minimize misinformation's impact on progress.

Combating Misinformation

Trying to combat misinformation is no easy matter. As I mentioned earlier in Chapter 5, people are prone to confirmation bias; they seek out information that supports. So, how can you combat misinformation? Lewandowsky et al. (2012) found ways to debunk misinformation and created a nice summary of their research (see Figure 33.1) on what deliverers of information can do.

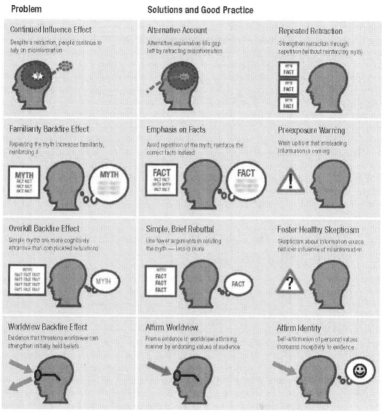

From the article: Misinformation and Its Correction: Continued Influence and Successful Debiasing by Lewandowsky et al. (2012). Psychological Science in the Public Interest, 13(3), 106-131.

Figure 33.1. Graphical summary of findings from the misinformation literature relevant to communication practitioners. The left-hand column summarizes the cognitive problems associated with misinformation, and the right-hand column summarizes the solutions. Figure is from the article by Lewandowsky et al. (2012).

To battle misinformation, you can:

- Provide alternative explanations. These alternative explanations fill in the gap that is left by retracted information.

- Repeat retractions without reinforcing the misinformation.

- Avoid too much repetition of the myth. Instead, reinforce the correct facts.

- In your communications, warn your audience when you are going to introduce the misinformation.

- Make your rebuttal brief and simple when refuting the misinformation.

- Promote skepticism. Focusing on the information source will reduce the impact of the misinformation.

- If your content is threatening to the worldview and values of your audience, present your point of view in a "worldview-affirming manner (e.g., by focusing on opportunities and potential benefits rather than risks and threats)."

Summary

Misinformation is all around us. Using the misinformation to form a belief can be detrimental not only to the holder of that belief but the people around them. Yet, once held, these beliefs can be very hard to change. Researchers have found several ways to combat misinformation. Try these approaches next time you are confronted with misinformation. Provide alternative explanations in a simple, concise way. Additionally, encourage skepticism in your audience. Perhaps skepticism is nothing more than what my nephew refers to as "the smell test." A tendency for your audience to adopt skepticism about information leads them to ask their own critical questions about claims that simply don't smell right. Finally, if your new information is threatening to your audience, try to focus your communication on how your information provides opportunities and potential benefits to your audience to move forward.

Chapter 34:
Customer
Experience
Management at
Oracle

*"The best scientist is open to experience and begins
with romance – the idea that anything is possible."*

Ray Bradbury

Oracle Corporation is the world's largest business software company. From its inception in 1977 to the present, Oracle has remained focused on continued innovation and helping its customers transform their businesses and achieve greater success. Oracle's customers use Oracle technology, applications, and services to build information systems that help them retain the value of existing investments; stay competitive in the current economic climate; cut costs and improve security; make compliance easier; and manage complex upgrades with fewer risks. These complete, open and integrated solutions enable customers to manage their business systems, information and customer relationships with reliable, secure and integrated technologies.

Customer centricity is a script that is supported from the top down, driving innovation on a daily basis. But innovation is not enough. As we will see by their adoption of several best practices, the core of Oracle's approach is looking at a holistic view of their customers. Oracle's Customer Experience Management (CEM) program uses different sources of customer data to drive deep insight into improving products, services and the processes that support them.

Oracle's global customer base is 390,000 and growing across all industries and company sizes. Revenues grew from US$22.4 billion in 2008 to US$37.1 billion in 2012.

Oracle's CEM program has come a long way in the last decade. As an example, in 2005, Oracle was executing multiple relationship surveys using various tools and methodologies, which made comparability across key customer segments extremely difficult. As mergers and acquisitions activity accelerated, the need to centralize surveys became clear and a requirement to providing stronger insight across their growing product footprint and expanding customer base. An enormous effort went into consolidating tools, standardizing methodologies, and globalizing processes. This in turn created opportunities to integrate processes and technologies, drive efficiencies into day-to-day operations, and create new demand for other business questions. While Oracle's

CEM program scope continues to expand, and operations continue to evolve, one central element remains the same: maintaining a centralized, coordinated approach for listening to, responding to and collaborating with customers.

Let us take a look at how Oracle structures their CEM program and see what kinds of activities they take in their approach. How Oracle operationalizes best practices will likely be different than many other companies. Like any company-wide initiative, you need to work within your company's constraints when considering how you will support CEM best practices. For example, while Oracle shares their customer feedback results across a variety of mediums, smaller companies will have fewer mediums to leverage. On the other hand, while CEM program differences may exist across companies, they share the same spirit in communicating results to the company. I provide the Oracle example to give you an inside look into how one major enterprise structures their CEM program.

Strategy/Governance

Oracle's success rests on having a clear understanding of their customers' needs and goals. They know that, to deliver an excellent customer experience, they have to provide industry leading solutions that solve customers' problems and are delivered by experts who are focused on their success. To accomplish this, Oracle uses customer feedback to help senior executives develop long-term strategic plans. The success of Oracle's CEM program is measured through account-specific relationship surveys. As Oracle President Mark Hurd reinforces, "We have a sophisticated account planning process that looks at the overall customer relationship across a rolling three-year time horizon. The account plan is a collaboratively developed approach to assuring the customer's longer-term objectives are met at the same time that Oracle's objectives are met."

Deep data governance is of central importance to Oracle. Oracle receives massive amounts of customer feedback annually. In fact, their surveys and panels alone capture over 550,000 responses each year. Consequently, proper program governance is necessary to ensure proper use of this complex web of customer data. Executives demand reliable, valid and useful information when they make their decisions, and data governance can go a long way to ensure they receive high-quality data to help them make the right decisions.

Oracle takes a centralized approach in the governance of their CEM program. Because of their size and diverse lines of business (LOB), this centralized approach provides them the needed control of CEM data with respect to what gets measured and how the data are used. The CEM program, however, is run in partnership with stakeholders across LOB to ensure a coordinated approach to capturing feedback, driving issues to resolution and integrating results with other customer data to ensure a holistic view of the customer experience (CX).

Driving a coordinated approach to CX reinforces shared accountability in ensuring customer success. Oracle's focus on the customer and their experience starts with top-level support. This executive support is manifested in different ways:

- Oracle Board of Directors includes a "Chief Customer Advocate" that regularly meets with customers and shares feedback results that reinforces customer perspectives.

- Executive Committee members meet with customers on a weekly basis to review customer metrics and use them to maintain continuity and reinforce the importance of customer focus.

- Mark Hurd, Oracle's President, hosts bi-quarterly global employee town hall meetings where he shares CEM program goals and results to highlight successes and to emphasize the importance of the customer to all employees. The meetings include interactive discussions and live Q&A.

- Customer feedback from account surveys

are embedded into strategic account plans that are shared with customers.

- Customer feedback results are communicated to Oracle's stakeholders in a variety of ways.

- Customer Feedback and Response Bulletin: A consolidated report containing key customer feedback across all channels, and Oracle's improvement initiatives and responses. Results are periodically reviewed by the Oracle Board of Directors and Executive Committee.

- Executive Readouts: Customer input collected across channels is integrated, analyzed and presented to senior executives across all geographies, LOB and development teams. These reports help the Executive Committee use customer feedback to compare products, services and account management activities, as well as implement improvement programs to address customer concerns.

- Hierarchical Reports: These reports are tailored for specific geographies, LOB and development teams to help them understand issues that are unique to them.

- Top Ten Themes: A list of top issues

affecting significant segments of Oracle's customer population, their experiences and the impact to Oracle, stemming from input across all customer programs.

Oracle's success is due, in large part, to their employees and their partners. Oracle's own studies have quantified the impact that employees and partners have on customer satisfaction and loyalty. As a result, through formal companywide programs, Oracle is always developing new ways to encourage and motivate employees and partners to be fully committed to helping customers succeed:

- Incentive, Compensation and Award Programs: Ensure employees and partners remain aligned with company objectives and customer success.

- Oracle PartnerNetwork (OPN) Diamond Partner program criteria include a threshold for ensuring excellent customer satisfaction through partners.

- Oracle Presidents Cup Awards recognize Oracle account teams and individuals that have contributed the most to customer satisfaction across all phases of account management.

- Oracle Service Excellence Awards allow customers to acknowledge the support and engineering teams that go above and beyond to address their issues and ensure their success.

- Oracle Pacesetter Awards highlight outstanding customer service.

As Luiz Meisler, EVP, Oracle Latin America states, "Our mission is to create value for our customers and establish long-term, strategic partnerships by combining complete industry solutions with specialized expertise to help customers address their business and technology needs and become more successful."

"The customer is at the very centre of everything we do in Oracle EMEA. They depend on us to provide the best possible advice and guidance to help them to do more in their businesses," says Loïc le Guisquet, EVP, Oracle EMEA.

Steve Au Yeung, EVP, Oracle Asia-Pacific said it best, "Focusing on customer success is embedded into everything we do."

Business Integration

Business integration means a couple of things. First, it means to incorporate customer feedback data into daily business processes. For example, call center agents, at a glance, can understand many different, yet complementary things about the customer: his prior interactions as well as his attitudes about those interactions. By integrating business data, you are able to provide the information your agents need to tailor their interactions with the customer. Knowing a premier caller (based on CRM system) had a recent negative experience (based on transactional survey), your call center agent's time might be better spent repairing the relationship rather than up-selling. Second, business integration means the process of integrating all business data to allow for a better understanding of large customer segments. Integration of business data is about applying appropriate analytics to these different business metrics (e.g., operational, financial, customer satisfaction/ loyalty) to uncover what is responsible for creating happy, loyal customers.

Here are some ways that Oracle ensures their CEM program (and its metrics) are integrated into other business data and processes.

- As a joint effort between Oracle and customer stakeholders, a performance scorecard is used to assess several dimensions of support delivery quality. The key metrics include measures of product quality, proactive performance, remediation, workload, and more. This scorecard provides the foundation for ongoing discussions between Oracle management and customers (via panels and other forums) on support performance and the impact of improvement initiatives.

- Customer information, survey samples, follow-up activities and results are securely stored in integrated Oracle databases.

- Oracle reports the information using their Customer Relationship Management (CRM) and Business Intelligence (BI) systems. Customer feedback responses requiring follow-up are automatically distributed to pre-determined employees empowered to take ownership, coordinate resources and outreach to the customer within 48 hours. Root cause identification and corrective action steps are tracked in Oracle CRM. Historical survey results are stored in Oracle CRM at the contact and account levels, and rolled up using Oracle BI to provide a single repository of role-based customer information for easy account team access.

- Anecdotal commentary and social media monitoring are tracked using Oracle Collective Intellect.

- All surveys are integrated into global list management policies to ensure privacy compliance at corporate and local levels.

Oracle continues to develop innovative new ways to create a work environment focused on the customer. Some examples include.

- MyIdeas@Work: This internal Web site allows employees to share ideas and vote on others' suggestions for driving innovation in support and enhancing the customer experience.

- Oracle Social Network (OSN): OSN is a broad range of social tools that helps employees collaborate in real-time across geographies and LOBs.

- Global Customer Care Community: This community includes representatives across the global organization who are responsible for executing customer programs within their span of responsibility. The community helps keep local activities aligned and provides a channel for input into systemic issues.

- Global Employee Survey: Oracle knows that the employee experience has a direct impact on the customer experience. To help monitor, manage and improve the employee experience, Oracle assesses employee satisfaction to help HR ensure employees are receiving the right tools and resources to deliver a great customer experience. Employee survey results are shared with the Executive Committee, and action plans are put in place to not only optimize retention and maximize productivity, but also increase end customer satisfaction.

Method/Reporting

The first piece of advice from Jeb Dasteel, Senior Vice President and Chief Customer Officer at Oracle is to "implement a cohesive customer feedback program before you do anything else. Demonstrating rigor and credibility in collection, analysis, and presentation of both quantitative and qualitative customer feedback creates a foundation of authority on which you can build all other customer programs."

Vehicles for capturing customer feedback include:

- Relationship Surveys: Oracle uses relationship surveys to evaluate account management and ongoing relationships. Focused on decision makers and influencers within their customer base, these surveys assess and trend experiences with account management, business practices, services and overall product perceptions across the ownership lifecycle. Post-merger surveys are also conducted to establish baselines, ease the on-boarding process and enable future trending.

- Product Panels: Oracle uses product surveys to assess satisfaction covering 15,000-plus products. Focused on end users, implementers and managers, these panels capture detailed and comparative feedback across the full Oracle product stack, and provide direct two-way communication between customers and Oracle Development General Managers.

- Transactional Surveys: Oracle has a set of transactional surveys that measure how well they execute specific business processes and obligations. Focused on customers at all levels, these surveys assess experiences with specific events, engagements and interactions across the customer lifecycle.

- Targeted Surveys: Tailored by job level and function given the objectives of the study, the aim of targeted surveys is to capture more detailed input on Oracle's top "customer feedback themes".

- Market Research: Coupled with surveys and panels, market research provides insight into market trends and competitive perspectives across our install base, prospects and partners.

Oracle tracks several key metrics using data from their customer feedback instruments. These metrics fall into three broad categories:

- Customer Loyalty: Customer loyalty is the "ultimate criterion" of Oracle's survey program and represents the extent to which their customers are advocates for the Oracle brand. The customer loyalty index (CLI) is a composite score that combines three questions: overall satisfaction, likelihood to recommend, and likelihood to continue purchasing.

- Customer Experience Metrics: These metrics reflect customer satisfaction across different touch points including product, support and account management.

- Value: The customer value metric reflects the perceived benefits customers receive from Oracle's solutions.

Oracle applies analytics to customer feedback to help identify key themes. They are much more confident with conclusions based on several lines of evidence than a single line of evidence. As such, customer feedback results from different sources are consolidated, including surveys, customer advisory boards and councils, user groups, executive escalations, root cause analysis, operational measures and financial metrics. Using these different sources of customer feedback, Oracle extracts and publicizes the ten "customer feedback themes" that have the greatest impact on CX and business results.

To address specific customer concerns, Oracle provides internal reporting tailored to employees' roles. Some of these reporting features reflect:

- Automated Alerts: If a customer answers a given survey question negatively (e.g., dissatisfied with their experience in products), automated alerts are generated and sent to pre-determined employees to enable immediate follow up and resolution of issues generated through customer surveys, escalations and visits. This approach ensures that Oracle addresses at-risk customers quickly.

- Account-level Reports: For large enterprise accounts that have multiple survey respondents (e.g., decision maker, decision influencer), survey results are aggregated for specific accounts and distributed to the account teams, executive sponsors and the customers. These reports are then incorporated into strategic account planning.

Applied Research

Oracle regularly conducts deep dive research using their customer experience data (see Chapter 28 to learn how Oracle organizes data). They accomplish this research by linking different metrics from disparate data sources together. Operational linkages, for example, help identify clear operational performance metrics (e.g., first call resolution, call handle time) that truly drive the customer experience; financial linkages allow Oracle to estimate the return on investment of different improvement initiatives; and constituency linkages allow Oracle to invest in effective employee experience programs that ultimately also enhance the customer experience.

Additionally, Oracle takes a longitudinal look at customer feedback data. Rather than solely relying on a cross-sectional view (all data from the same period), Oracle uses a time-series approach to identify cause and effect relationships among metrics, allowing them to make stronger predictive claims about the causes of customer satisfaction and loyalty.

As outlined in Chapter 28, Oracle combines metrics across a variety of different data silos to research many different types of questions. In one research endeavor, Oracle focused in on the support process. Toward that end, they integrated operational support data and end user experience with support to identify the call center metrics that drove caller satisfaction. Additionally, they integrated different types of survey data to examine whether end user support experience (those who used the applications) was related to their management's experience (decision makers who purchased the applications).

Oracle found that end user satisfaction with support is stable over time; when an end user has a positive experience with Oracle Support, they are more likely to be satisfied with future support experiences.

Also, end user satisfaction, in turn, impacts the perceptions of the end user's management. Accounts with end users who are satisfied with their support experience have executives who report satisfaction with Oracle Support overall. End user satisfaction had a downstream positive influence on decision maker and influencer perceptions of the support experience. Based on the findings of this research, Oracle identified and targeted improvement initiatives in Oracle Hardware Support, leading to increases in overall satisfaction with Support.

In another research project, Oracle investigated the longitudinal effects of community interaction and static knowledge search in reducing the need for service. Clickstream data was used to capture community participation behavior from My Oracle Support (MOS) members and merged with Service Request (SR) information. Customer feedback about SR satisfaction In another research project, Oracle investigated the longitudinal effects of community interaction and static knowledge search in reducing the need for service. Clickstream data was used to capture community participation behavior from My Oracle Support (MOS) members and merged with Service Request (SR) information. Customer feedback about SR satisfaction and community satisfaction were merged with these data. Results showed that, after controlling for previous SR activity, live community interaction with other participants had a significant positive impact in reducing the customer's need for service in future time periods compared to static knowledge search. This research allowed Oracle to predict the impact of community interaction on cost of service and customer satisfaction. The analysis helped Oracle focus investments in areas that improve community interaction and reduce the need for service, while also expanding knowledge base capabilities to enable self-service resolution when support was required.

Over the past 3 years, Oracle has been conducting a number of joint research activities with its user groups worldwide, and sharing the results collaboratively with user group leaders, who in turn provide input into potential action plans and strategies. The results of these studies show that customers who are involved with Oracle's independent user groups are significantly more satisfied and more likely to recommend Oracle than their non-user group peers. It appears that customers who are more engaged (e.g., participate in user groups) receive greater value from their investments and, consequently, are happier with Oracle's solutions.

Impact of Oracle's CEM Program

It is one thing to have a CEM program. It is another thing to track its impact on customers and your business. Oracle monitors and tracks their financial and CEM program metrics to ensure that they are delivering on their promise to help customers succeed. As a result, Oracle reaps the benefits financially: in fiscal year 2012, Oracle's annual revenue reached US$37.1B, up from US$11.1B in FY05.

During the same timeframe, Oracle has seen significant improvements in its CX metrics. First, the Customer Loyalty Index (CLI) has been steadily rising. This increase in customer loyalty is paralleled by improvements in satisfaction in other key metrics like perceived value, quality of relationships and support. Not surprisingly, during this same period, the time to resolve customer-specific issues identified through surveys has declined three fold.

Looking regionally at customer decision makers and

influencers, a number of statistically significant increases in satisfaction with relationship-based measures are reported year-over year. These increases align directly with programs architected globally and implemented locally, empowering account teams to customize engagement under a common framework (See Figure 34.1).

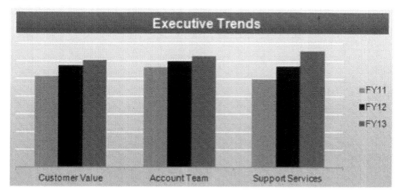

Figure 34.1. Trends for some of Oracle's key metrics show improvements

When looking at Oracle's top segment of customers (e.g., Key Accounts), significant gains in satisfaction are seen as the result of the development of the Key Account Director role (KAD). These gains for Key Accounts are higher than the general population, confirming the increased value of the KAD program (See Figure 34.2).

Figure 34.2. Comparisons across accounts show impact of Oracle's Key Account Director (KAD) program on key customer metrics.

Chapter 35: Assessing your CEM Program

"If you don't know where you're headed, you'll probably end up someplace else."

Douglas J. Eder

The way you structure your CEM program impacts its success. If you are a CEM professional who manages customer feedback for your company, you can take the Customer Feedback Program Diagnostic **(CFPD)** to determine if your CEM program adopts best practices. This brief assessment process can help your company:

- identify your CEM program's strengths and weaknesses

- understand how to improve your CEM program

- facilitate your customer experience improvement efforts

- increase customer loyalty

Upon completion of this 10-minutes assessment, you will receive immediate feedback on your company's CEM program. To take the CFPD, go here: http://businessoverbroadway.com/resources/self-assessment-survey.

Chapter 36: Additional Readings

"The more that you read, the more things you will know. The more that you learn, the more places you'll go."

Dr. Seuss

References

Allen, M.J., & Yen, W. M. (2002). Introduction to Measurement Theory. Long Grove, IL: Waveland Press.

Anderson, E. W., Fornell, C., & Mazvancheryl, S. K. (2004). Customer satisfaction and shareholder value. Journal of Marketing, 68 (October), 72-185.

Cronbach, L. J. (1951). Coefficient alpha and the internal structure of tests. Psychometrika, 16(3), 297-334.

Fornell, C., Mithas, S., Morgensen, F. V., Krishan, M. S. (2006). Customer satisfaction and stock prices: High returns, low risk. Journal of Marketing, 70 (January), 1-14.

Gruca, T. S., & Rego, L. L. (2005). Customer satisfaction, cash flow, and shareholder value. Journal of Marketing, 69 (July), 115-130.

Hayes, B.E. (2011). Lessons in loyalty. Quality Progress, March, 24-31.

Hayes, B.E., Goodden, R., Atkinson, R., Murdock, F. & Smith, D. (2010). Where to Start: Experts weight in on what all of us can learn from Toyata's challenges. Quality Progress, April, 16-23.

Hayes, B. E. (2009). Beyond the ultimate question: A systematic approach to improve customer loyalty. Quality Press. Milwaukee, WI.

Hayes, B. E. (2008a). Measuring customer satisfaction and loyalty: Survey design, use and statistical analysis methods (3rd ed.). Quality Press. Milwaukee, WI.

Hayes, B. E. (2008b). Customer loyalty 2.0: The Net Promoter Score debate and the meaning of customer loyalty, Quirk's Marketing Research Review, October, 54-62.

Hayes, B. E. (2008c). The true test of loyalty. Quality Progress. June, 20-26.

Ironson, G.H., Smith, P.C., Brannick, M.T., Gibson W.M. & Paul, K.B. (1989). Construction of a "Job in General" scale: A comparison of global, composite, and specific measures. Journal of Applied Psychology, 74, 193-200.

Keiningham, T. L., Cooil, B., Andreassen, T.W., & Aksoy, L. (2007). A longitudinal examination of net promoter and firm revenue growth. Journal of Marketing, 71 (July), 39-51.

Morgan, N.A. & Rego, L.L. (2006). The value of different customer satisfaction and loyalty metrics in predicting business performance. Marketing Science, 25(5), 426-439.

Netpromoter.com (2007). Homepage.

Nunnally, J. M. (1978). Psychometric Theory, Second Edition. New York, NY. McGraw-Hill.

Reichheld, F. F. (2003). The One Number You Need to Grow. Harvard Business Review, 81 (December), 46-54.

Reichheld, F. F. (2006). The ultimate question: driving good profits and true growth. Harvard Business School Press. Boston.

24906951R00184

Made in the USA
Lexington, KY
06 August 2013